Business Strategy Roadmap

For Better and Faster Results

William Nana Wiafe II

Bloomington, IN

Milton Keynes, UK

AuthorHouse™
1663 Liberty Drive, Suite 200
Bloomington, IN 47403
www.authorhouse.com
Phone: 1-800-839-8640

AuthorHouse™ UK Ltd.
500 Avebury Boulevard
Central Milton Keynes, MK9 2BE
www.authorhouse.co.uk
Phone: 08001974150

First published by AuthorHouse 4/4/2006

ISBN: 1-4208-6918-3 (sc)

Printed in the United States of America
Bloomington, Indiana

This book is printed on acid-free paper.

Table of Contents

Dedication

To my wife Catherine, and to my daughters Jessica and Stephanie, I dedicate this book to you. I thank you greatly for your patience, understanding, and support throughout my writing and re-writing of this book.

Tribute

This book is a tribute to my father, Nana Wiafe II, the late King of a state in Ghana, to my mother, and to my brothers and sisters.

Preface

It was a pleasure researching and writing this book. Numerous sources of reference have been acknowledged in the reference section of this book. Dr. Gurprit Kindra, Dr. Jonathan Calof, Mr. Pierre Bergeron, and Dr. John Cuillard (professors at The University of Ottawa (U of O) School of Management) and Mr. Edward Pascal (former Director of the MBA program at U of O) have been great source of inspiration and valued colleagues. My sincere thanks go to Mr. Clifford T. Lebarron (current Director, National Bank of Canada and former Vice-President, RoyNat) for his sincerity, honesty, and courage. He is a wonderful role model. I thank Mr. Mel Skinner (former Assistant Deputy Minister, and current Vice-President - Canada Mortgage and Housing Corporation) for the opportunity to work on his projects and for his guidance.

I must express my warm thanks to Author House for accepting to publish this book and, to the entire team at Author House, particularly Jennifer Brandt, Valerie Raney, Lesley Bolton, and Brad Tirey. They have been pleasant and professional in all my dealings with them. I thank the editors for their interest and their suggestions. Many thanks to the book design team, especially, Matthew Monroe, and Tony Barger. The services that I received from the Author House were exceptional and I look forward to a long relationship.

Picture credits

I thank Portrait Now for granting me the permission to reproduce my portrait for this book. Sincere thanks to Daniel Benoit who took my photograph.

Author's message to readers

This book is sold with the understanding that the author is not rendering professional services on the specific circumstances of individuals or organizations. The author offers no guarantees or warrantees of any kind. Readers should be aware that the Internet references might have disappeared or changed after the publication of this book.

Reasons to Buy This Book

Is your business facing competition? Do you want to achieve better and faster results? If your objective is to increase market share, achieve higher growth, earn higher profits, achieve higher overall performance, or earn above-average returns, this book is for you. This book is written for those who want a bigger share of the pie.

In today's hyper-competitive world, business strategy is no longer something that can be pushed to the sidelines and revisited at a convenient time in the future. Constant demands, business challenges, and competitive pressures have made a business strategy a necessity for survival and sustainability.

There are countless reasons to buy this book. Some of the key benefits of this book are:

- The book brings everything you need to think about to develop an effective strategy together in one place.
- It is full of illustrations that you can use in your business to help you make the right strategy decisions.
- It will coach you towards developing a strategy mindset for dealing with business challenges.
- The book is practical and is intended for those who want to achieve higher overall performance, higher growth, higher profits, or increased market share.

- The book goes straight to the heart of business strategy without the often-confusing jargon.
- Executives, managers, and business owners who read this book will increase their value to their firms or their organizations.
- The book provides executives, managers, and business owners with strategy decision tools to make the right choices and achieve the desired strategy objectives.
- The book acts as a **business strategy coach** for firms, executives, managers, and business owners. It is like having a personal trainer to coach you in developing an effective strategy for your organization.
- This book is for those who do not accept the status quo and know that they deserve better.
- You can start applying the knowledge from this book today and start reaping the benefits.
- This book will coach you in assessing and managing risks associated with business strategy project for better results.
- It will coach you on how to assess your internal environment, external environment, and industry environment so that you can identify competitive threats and minimize or eliminate them, identify opportunities and take advantage of them, identify weaknesses and turn them into opportunities, and identify strengths and capitalize on them.

- The **Strategy Roadmap** and the **Strategy Navigator** together, will coach you towards achieving better and faster results. Developing and implementing an effective business strategy has never been simpler.

More importantly, the book will guide you in setting the strategic direction for your business or organization. It will also help you get there.

The book offers flexibility to managers, executives, and business owners in developing their individualized strategies that can be tailored to their own circumstances. It is not a one-size-fits-all approach to business strategy. It provides room for creativity.

How to order from the Publisher

To order copies of this book in bulk, call Author House at 1-888-519-5121 or visit www.globastrat.com.

Chapter 1

Your business is booming and you are thinking of expanding, but you do not know what to do next. You want better and faster results, and you are wondering how to achieve them. You want to increase your market share, earn higher profits, achieve higher growth and performance, or earn above-average returns, but cannot seem to put things together to achieve any of them. Your business faces competition and you do not know what to do next.

Well, you are not alone. These are only a few of the many realities people in business face. They are only a sample of the numerous challenges that keep CEOs, business owners, and senior managers awake at night. Regardless of your type of business — law firm, real estate firm, manufacturing firm, medical practice, hospital and clinic, consulting firm, accounting firm, technology firm, service business, or not-for-profit business — every business needs to do better. Regardless of which business you are in, you deserve a bigger share of the pie.

Perhaps you are wondering how you can do better in your business. You are asking yourself what else you need to think of in order to improve your overall performance. You have done everything you could think of but things do not seem to improve. You cannot seem to put your finger on what specifically you need to do to turn things around for the better.

This book is like a one-stop shop to provide what you need to know and do to achieve better and faster results. Business owners, CEOs, and other managers often obtain advice from people in specific areas such as accounting, production, finance, and so on. Very rarely do they get advice covering their external and internal environments or industry factors, all of which affect their results. The book assembles in one place what you need to know and do to formulate, develop, and implement a strategy that meets your needs and circumstances.

In today's global and hyper-competitive world, strategy is no longer something that is overhead that can be pushed to the sidelines and revisited at a convenient time in the future, or be discarded as irrelevant and useless academic claptrap. The increasing reliance on global trade agreements, the use of e-business, Internet, e-commerce, and other technology applications to provide a wide range of business solutions has meant that CEOs, business owners, and other senior managers have to have a strategy to stay a step ahead of competitors.

Constant demands, business challenges, and competitive pressures on businesses have made strategy a business necessity that contributes to business survival and sustainability. The Strategy Roadmap for Better and Faster Results is for those who seriously want to increase profits, growth and market share, earn above-average returns, or achieve higher overall performance in this era of global competition and increasing hyper-competitiveness. The book is for those who do not accept the status quo or mediocre performance results and are looking for better and faster ways to achieve positive results.

Strategy addresses the fundamental question of how a firm achieves above-average returns, higher market share, higher growth, and better and faster results. Although the question may seem quite straightforward, answers are by no means simple. Attempts to explain how a firm achieves above-average returns, higher market share, or higher growth can be found in economics and business strategy literature. The literature is filled with sometimes intimidating and confusing terminology. In many instances, this terminology only makes sense to those who work in the field of business strategy, such as academics and consultants, to the chagrin of business owners, managers, and executives.

Answers to the question are rooted in strategy analysis, the business environment, management decisions, an awareness of strategy landscape, and a systematic (not a scattered) approach to strategy. Piecing together the many dimensions of strategy requires skills and knowledge. An effective strategy focuses on things that are ultimately important to a firm, such as making more money.

Closing the skills and knowledge gap is the necessary first step to understanding, formulating, developing, and implementing a business strategy that will produce better and faster performance results. When managers and executives are skilled and knowledgeable in business strategy, they can achieve above-average returns. More importantly, it is only when the skills and knowledge are successfully applied that a firm begins to achieve above-average performance and above-average returns. This book challenges you to ask yourself the very fundamental question of how to achieve better and faster results.

Developing a complete understanding of business strategy is like finding your way out of a maze. Terms such as business unit strategy, strategic business unit, corporate strategy, strategic management, competitive advantage, core competencies, strategic intent, and sustainable competitive advantage are but a few examples of how strategy dazzles and dazes managers and executives. There are many different definitions of strategy, which add to more confusion and complexity.

The aim of this book is not to debate what strategy is or is not. The objective of this book is to assemble strategy frameworks, models, and knowledge in one place so that firms can use them to develop a business strategy to help them achieve above-average performance, higher profitability, growth, and market share. This is a one-stop shop for aspiring managers, incumbent managers, and executives of organizations, as well as business owners.

The **Strategy Roadmap (SR)** is the most distinguishing attribute of this book. It provides a guidance system to demystify business strategy. It is presented using a project approach so that it is simpler, clearer to understand, and easy to work with in order to achieve better and faster results. The SR presents strategy in a structured, systematic, and methodical manner without diminishing creativity in the thought processes for strategy. It challenges managers or executives to develop a business strategy using the elements or the components of the SR so that it meets the unique and specific competitive circumstances of their firm.

The SR allows managers and executives to see at a glance what they need to know and consider when developing a business strategy. This reduces the complexities, confusion, and mystique associated with business strategy. The SR makes it simpler to develop a personalized business strategy for action. The Strategy Roadmap is presented in chapter eleven.

In a changing and challenging competitive marketplace, firms must set objectives to achieve higher profitability, growth, market share, returns, or overall performance. Some firms succeed in achieving their objectives, but others do not. While the reasons for failure or success are many and complex, one thing is clear. There is a link between business strategy (written or unwritten) and a firm's overall performance. With the ever-changing business environment, the dynamics of the market forces, and the challenges of competitive forces, it becomes ever so important for firms to have a well-thought-out and effective business strategy. Managers and executives must be equipped with the knowledge and skills to develop and apply business strategy in a way that maximizes the value of the firm. They must be able to make management decisions grounded on solid strategy analysis that aims at improving profitability, growth, and overall performance.

Contrary to the conventional wisdom, the goal of business strategy is not necessarily to beat a competitor. Beating a competitor who is not making money is not a victory at all. The goal of business strategy is to make more money over and above what the industry makes on average. That is, to earn above-average performance or above-average returns in the industry in which a firm operates. A firm uses business strategy to achieve higher market share, growth, or overall profitability. In so doing, a firm can increase its chances of achieving above-average performance within the industry in which it operates.

The business strategy environment is complex, consisting of industry environment forces, external environment forces, and internal environment forces. These forces can affect firms both negatively and positively. They can limit a firm's ability to increase profitability, market share, growth, or overall performance. External forces, internal forces, and forces specific to an industry can have a tremendous influence on a firm's ability to earn above-average performance. The positive side to this is that they provide the motivation for firms to work even harder and search for better ways to compete to win. The same business environment that affects firms negatively can also be a source of opportunities. Figure 1 shows a firm's business strategy environment in a nutshell.

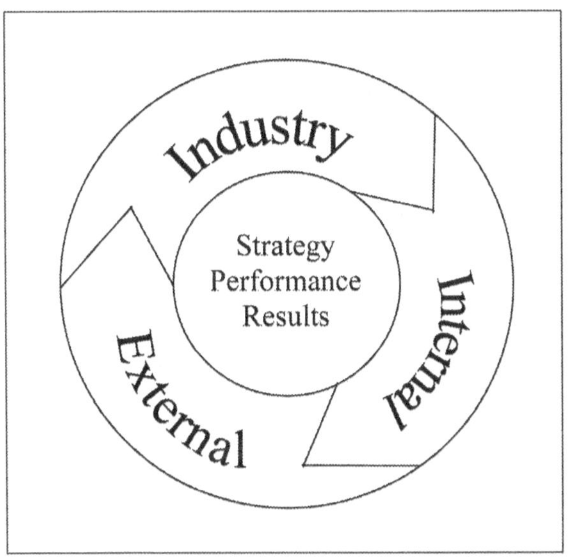

Figure 1: Business Strategy Environment

A well-thought-out business strategy is the answer to competing to win. This book presents models, tools, techniques, and frameworks that will enable a firm to focus on achieving better and faster performance results. The **Strategy Roadmap (SR)** offers the means to achieve higher profitability, market share, growth, and better and faster overall performance.

In developing a business strategy, a firm must be able to identify its strengths and be capable of capitalizing on them. It must identify weaknesses and minimize or eliminate them. It must also recognize threats and minimize or eliminate them. It must identify opportunities and seize them. The ability of a firm to minimize threats and weaknesses and capitalize on strengths and opportunities is at the heart of business strategy.

A firm is successful if it increases its growth, profitability, market share, or overall performance; or if it earns above-average performance. A firm must show how it intends to achieve above-average performance. The models and approaches presented in this book allow a manager or an executive to develop an increased understanding of their firm's environment, increase their skills and knowledge of business strategy, and make informed decisions about how to increase growth, overall performance, profitability, or market share. Such an understanding and knowledge will allow the manager or executive to move a firm in the desired strategic direction.

The book will benefit business owners, managers, executives, presidents, vice-presidents, chief executive officers, chief operating officers, and those who are responsible for strategy. After all, these individuals have a stake in the business and are ultimately responsible for a firm's performance, attractiveness of the firm to investors, and the continued viability of the firm. They are responsible for management decisions, financial decisions, operational decisions, and in setting strategic directions for their firms. In short, they are responsible for the firm's success in achieving above-average performance or above-average returns. Consultants, business professors,

MBA students and other business students, government officials, and not-for-profit organizations will find this book beneficial. MBA programs and other business programs can use this book to supplement recommended textbooks. This serves as a compendium to strategic management and strategic policy textbooks or as a quick reference for business case analysis. This book is one of a kind in demystifying business strategy and making it much simpler to develop a business strategy that meets individual circumstances. Where possible, it uses diagrams, exhibits, and mini cases to improve learning.

The book is written in plain language and, will benefit those who have managerial responsibilities but do not have time to pursue formal business degrees or diplomas, and yet need something quick and simple to get the job done. It is invaluable, whether you work for a not-for-profit organization or a business corporation. Today many not-for-profit organizations, including church ministries, political parties, and business enterprises, find themselves in competition with one another for customers. Therefore, business strategy is no longer something for large business corporations alone. This book will guide small and medium-size enterprises, not-for-profit organizations, as well as political campaign managers and campaign executives who want to develop a strategy visual map and a strategy mindset to win.

Welcome to the world of business strategy

After reading this book you will

- acquire a strategy mindset to meet business challenges
- be able to create a visual and mental map for developing an effective business strategy
- gain an understanding and knowledge of business strategy
- have the ability to develop an effective business strategy to achieve better and faster results for your organization

The book

- brings everything you need to know in one place to develop and implement a business strategy for better and faster results
- goes straight to the heart of strategy to demystify and simplify business strategy so that it is easier to understand and apply
- uses a project approach that walks you through business strategy development step-by-step towards achieving better and faster results;
- coaches you towards achieving higher profits, better market share, higher growth, better overall profitability, or higher above-average returns

PART I

Business Strategy Environment

Chapter 2

External Environment

No firm can evade the impact of the forces or factors within its environment. While most of these factors are uncontrollable, a firm can influence their impact, if the firm anticipates occurrences far in advance. This chapter focuses on the external environment. Subsequent chapters will discuss other forces within a firm's environment.

Some external forces or factors can pose threats to firms. Threats can seriously hamper the ability of a firm to compete effectively. They can diminish a firm's performance, profitability, market share, or growth. The net result is an unfavourable impact on the firm's resources and financial viability, which can lead to a corporate takeover or bankruptcy.

However, external environment is not all about threats. It can provide a firm with many opportunities to improve performance, profitability, growth, or market share. Some opportunities can increase a firm's ability to compete more successfully. When a firm is able to exploit opportunities, it can substantially increase performance or market share, or earn above-average profitability within its industry.

Depending on circumstances, external factors can affect firms positively or negatively. For example, when there is high unemployment some firms can see this as an opportunity to lower their labour cost. Similarly, a lower Canadian dollar in relation to the U.S. dollar can spell opportunity for Canadian firms who export their products to the United States. On the other hand, a lower Canadian dollar can have a negative impact on firms who import products from the United States. Firms facing this situation could see their profits eroded by the exchange rate differential.

External Environment Factors

External environment forces are numerous. Some are:

- Population changes
- Lifestyle changes
- New technologies
- Government regulations
- Change in consumer tastes
- High unemployment
- Legal actions
- Lower disposable income
- Slow economic activity
- Lower or higher exchange rates
- Cost of borrowing money
- Inflation
- Economic growth

As can be seen, these forces or factors are many and a framework to identify and present them in an organized manner is necessary. This permits their use in strategic analysis and the development of a business strategy.

A framework for analyzing the external environment is GST-PLEDGE. The GST-PLEDGE stands for global, social, technological, political, legal, economic, demographic, government actions, and ecology (environment) factors as shown in Figure 2. These GST-PLEDGE factors allow firms to take a closer look at the outside world in an organized manner.

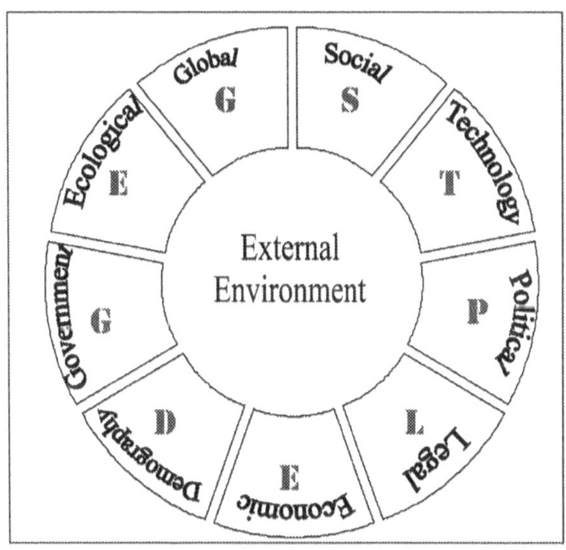

Figure 2: The GST-PLEDGE

The GST-PLEDGE illustrates dynamic and uncontrollable environmental forces or factors that can affect all firms whether directly or indirectly, positively or negatively. The extent of their impact will vary from firm to firm. Some firms are able to withstand the impact of the GST-PLEDGE factors better than others. Other firms merely collapse and fold like aluminium tin cans. From time to time, a firm has to identify the GST-PLEDGE factors and assess their potential impact. Doing so allows the firm to be better prepared to take the necessary actions to deal with the factors more effectively rather than experiencing surprises.

Global Factors

The expansion of the European Union, the growth in the demand of petroleum, the spread of terrorism, severe acute respiratory syndrome (SARS), and mad cow disease (BSE), have one thing in common. They are global factors that can have drastic effects on countries, firms, consumers, the economy, and people.

In May 2004, the European Union (EU) increased its membership by ten, from fifteen to twenty-five member states. Why should firms, particularly those in the EU, take notice of the expansion of the EU? Because this opens up economic development opportunities for firms as the new members will strive to catch up with existing members in the EU. This in turn can lead to international development project opportunities and create demand for experts in certain sectors of their economy. Competition would increase as new firms emerge from the new member states. Exports and imports would increase in the EU with the expansion of its members. The labour pool in incumbent member countries would expand as immigrants from the new member countries seek employment opportunities throughout the European Union.

In another example, the continued growth in demand for petroleum and rapid economic growth in some economies would continue to push up petroleum prices. As the demand for petroleum increases, production of petroleum would no longer be able to satisfy this growth in demand, at least not in the short term. This would create a shortage in the petroleum market as supply fails to match demand in the short run. Firms would no longer enjoy lower production costs as petroleum prices rise. Consumers would pay higher prices as the cost of production increases since producers pass their costs on to consumers. Some firms (such as airlines) that use petroleum as inputs to provide services to their customers generally take the brunt of petroleum price increases. The cost to travel by airplane or by automobile would continue to rise. With the rising petroleum and gas prices, consumers would seek an alternative way to travel and motorists would demand more energy-saving vehicles.

The September 11, 2001 terrorist attack in the United States created enormous economic havoc. The attack affected not only firms in the U.S. but also firms in other countries, particularly those who do business directly or indirectly with the U.S. The flow of goods between Canada and the United States came to a grinding halt as delays occurred at border crossings because of heightened security. Demand for security products and services increased as the race to protect citizens and commerce dominated news headlines. Security in both Canadian and American federal government buildings, airports, and border crossings became a major preoccupation. As terrorism continues to occupy the minds of citizens, countries, and consumers, firms are finding innovative ways to protect people, property, and commerce.

On the other hand, the recent outbreak of severe acute respiratory syndrome (SARS) and mad cow disease generated a negative economic impact for Canada. In Toronto, the impact of SARS brought the tourism industry to its knees. Hotel occupancy rates in Toronto fell to an all-time low. Many hotels had to lay off their employees. Fewer people visited Toronto because organizers cancelled previously scheduled international events. The World Health Organization (WHO) issued a travel advisory warning to citizens of other countries to avoid traveling to Toronto unless it was necessary to do so. The outbreak of mad cow disease in Alberta had a similar negative impact on the Canadian economy. The United States, Mexico, and Japan banned the importation of cattle and beef from Canada. The ban severely affected the Canadian cattle industry.

It will take many years to assess the full impact of the south Asia tsunami, which occurred in the Indian Ocean, on December 26, 2004. Thousands of people died or were washed away into the sea. Bandeh Aceh, Indonesia, and Sri Lanka were among the countries that were most devastated by the tsunami. Disease, human suffering, environmental, and ecological effects are only a few examples of its impact. The tsunami will create challenges and opportunities for governments and businesses to do the right thing as the economic and human impact continue to unfold.

These examples demonstrate how global factors create opportunities and challenges for firms. They can have negative or positive impacts on firms, countries, and consumers. Some global factors can create havoc and cripple the economies of countries and firms within them. Yet, in some instances, global factors can create opportunities for firms and industries to thrive. Firms that ignore global factors do so at their peril, as they can influence a firm's profitability, market share, and performance. Close monitoring of these factors is a business imperative and they must always be on a firm's radar.

Social Factors

Firms face many changes in their external environment. Social changes reflect social attitudes towards products and services of firms, which in turn affect demand for firms' products and services. Social changes and attitudes can also affect the firms' cost of production. These have the effect of making firms re-think the way they produce products or services. For example, the desire of parents to find something more convenient than cloth diapers was enough to cause Proctor & Gamble to respond by producing disposable diapers as part of its line of baby products to fulfill this parental need. With the aid of modern technology, Proctor & Gamble was able to dominate this market segment with its high quality and, low-cost branded disposable diapers (Pampers) for years.

Newspapers report on changing social attitudes every day. Just like with global factors, firms that ignore social factors do so at their own risk. Social factors affect business performance. Demand for business services or products has a direct impact on sales volume and consequently on revenues and performance of a particular industry sector. For example, in Canada there is a demographic trend towards an aging population. This creates opportunities for businesses and entrepreneurs to develop services and products to meet the needs of this segment of the population. Similarly, the number of ethnic families in Canada is on the rise. Television broadcasting services, including Planet Africa Television, are responding to this market segment with multicultural or diversity programming.

On the other hand, the low birth rate in Canada is a signal to firms that this is a declining market segment. It signals fierce competition among firms in the youth market because of the dwindling number of consumers. Social factors create opportunities and challenges to which firms have to pay attention in developing their business strategy. Which social factors have a direct or indirect impact on your business? Do they have the potential to impact performance and profitability? What opportunities or challenges do these social factors bring to your business?

Technological Factors

The impact of technology is felt everywhere. The use of technology is on the streets, in homes, and in offices. In almost every corner of the globe, one can find Internet applications, cell phones, laptops, or desktop computers. Many businesses nowadays are using technology in many instances.

One industry where technology is making an impact is the music industry. Technology allows consumers to obtain their favourite music free, or at a bare minimum fee, from peer-to-peer (P2P) networks. People share music files using these peer-to-peer networks with the help of an Internet application. Consumers can now order their music online from sites such as Amazon, Barnes & Noble, and Chapters. This method of music acquisition has an impact on the music industry. It is certainly different from the traditional way of creating and distributing music.

In the airline industry, technology has allowed airlines to move from handwritten reservation systems to an automated passenger reservation system. Semi-Automatic Business Research Environment, known as the SABRE system, enabled American Airlines to automate its passenger reservation system and allowed the airline to reduce its staff cost by 30 percent.

Wal-Mart, for example, has used technology as part of its business strategy for years to dominate its industry. There are numerous firms, which have been impacted, positively or negatively, by technology.

What is the impact of technology on your firm? Has your firm considered using technology to increase or dominate its market segment? Is the firm using technology to increase its overall profitability and performance?

Political Factors

Political factors affect a firm's profitability and performance. All firms and industries operate in a political environment. Politicians generally debate policies before they become law. Laws about competition, taxation, and other business laws regulate the behaviour or conduct of businesses.

Pressure groups, lobbyists, and other interest groups also influence politicians. Take as an example a developer who plans to build condominium housing for upscale senior citizens. Assume that the government owns this piece of property and is willing to sell this property to the developer. Pressure groups and lobbyists form to stop the sale of the property to the developer. They claim that it would be better to reserve the property for parks and recreation or for other leisure activities. The politicians debate the issues and cast their votes. How the vote turns out would definitely affect the developer's bottom line, positively or negatively.

Consider again the mad cow incident in the province of Alberta (Canada) and its impact on the cattle business. While this incident started as a provincial health and safety issue, it ballooned into an international political and diplomatic event, leaving businesses and politicians frustrated. Businesses in the cattle industry lost thousands of dollars because of the political and diplomatic impasse between Canada, the United States, Japan, and other countries who refused to import Canadian cattle.

Legal Factors

Legal factors can manifest themselves in many ways. For example, consumers can bring legal action against a company. A supplier or a property owner can take legal action against a firm and, if successful, put it out of business.

Firms must respect laws such as competition law, trade law, contract law, and intellectual property law if they are to avoid lawsuits. Intellectual property laws include copyrights, patents, trademarks, and industrial designs, which protect owners of these intellectual properties from those who might infringe on them or abuse their use. This is because intellectual properties can be a source of competitive advantage. Firms usually take legal action against their competitors in defence of these intellectual property rights. There are also laws that are specific to an industry such as, transportation, health, finance, and insurance laws.

Legal action against a firm has the potential to drain a firm's resources, decrease profitability, and even put a firm out of business. This was evident in the lawsuit against Microsoft under the competition laws of the United States. While Microsoft survived the lawsuit, the company suffered bad publicity. Mr. Bill Gates had to take time away from his regular duties to prepare for his appearance before U.S. federal officials. This was a drain on the company's resources, particularly due to legal fees. This also affected Microsoft's share prices.

In Canada, federal, provincial, and municipal levels of government make applicable laws and regulations. It is important to be aware of these legal factors or laws that affect businesses. For example, it is wise to consider your financial capability to compete when faced with a legal action, which could result in draining a firm's financial resources. Some firms set aside cash reserves to deal with such eventualities. Is your firm knowledgeable of the applicable laws, such as the competition laws and, laws specific to the industry in which the firm operates?

Economic Factors

Economics plays a major role in the performance of firms. Since the times of Adam Smith, David Ricardo, Jean-Baptiste Say, Ivring Fisher, Jean Maynard Keynes, and Milton Friedman, economists continue to influence public policy and economic decisions. Decisions about employment, exchange rates, interest rates, poverty, health, pollution, trade, and education are but a few examples of the influence economics has on public policy decisions. Each of these decisions has an economic impact on a firm's profitability and performance.

A rise or fall in the value of the dollar affects some industries more than others. An increase in the value of the Canadian dollar compared to the U.S. dollar affects firms in Canada that export lumber, cattle, and beef to the U.S. A higher Canadian dollar compared to American dollar can make Canadian products more expensive and less attractive to U.S. importers. Conversely, a lower Canadian dollar can make Canadian goods more attractive to the U.S. market.

In the same way, exchange rate fluctuations affect the tourism industry. A lower Canadian dollar compared to the American dollar, the Euro, or the British pound can attract tourists from these countries to Canada. This can have a potential to boost occupancy rates of hotels and the financial performance of firms in the airline industry. However, the opposite effect can occur should the Canadian dollar rise in value compared to other countries' currencies.

A rise in interest rates increases the cost of borrowing money. A higher cost of borrowing money affects a firm's ability to produce at a lower cost. The cost of keeping and paying employees can lead to lay-offs, especially when the cost of borrowing rises. This can cause the level of unemployment to rise, resulting in people having less money to spend on consumer goods. Lower demand translates into lower profits for firms.

Demand for products and services influences the quantity of products a firm is willing to produce and the price it will charge buyers. Supply and demand is at the heart of strategy for any business or organization. They affect resource allocation and strategy decisions. The amount or quantity a firm produces will depend on the resources available to the firm, and the quantity consumers are willing to buy. These affect a firm's profitability, performance, and market share.

Equally important to firms are economic indicators. Economic indicators are economic information, which give an indication of how well or badly the economy is doing, and how well it is expected to do in the future. There are several economic indicators. Some of them are:

- Consumer Price Index (CPI)
- Gross Domestic Product (GDP)
- Producer Price Index (PPI)
- Employment Indicators
- Retail Sales Index (RSI)
- Consumer Confidence Index

Economic indicators are important to consider when developing a business strategy. For example, it may not be wise to increase production or expand when consumer confidence is low and when the economy is heading into a recession. Similarly, a retailer would be prudent not to overstock inventory when the retail sales index is expected to be low. Economic indicators are used to forecast when the economy is heading towards a recession, a slump, or a recovery. In addition to the above economic indicators, other economic indicators exist that are specific to different industries. What economic indicators are specific to your firm's industry?

Demographic Factors

Demographic information is one of the essential pieces of information that a firm needs in deciding which particular segment of the market to focus on or serve. Exhibit 1 shows some examples of demographic factors, which affect a firm's performance, profitability, and market share.

Exhibit 1: Demographic factors

- income
- gender
- occupation
- family size
- home ownership
- religion
- education
- age
- ethnic orgin
- marital status

Firms can improve sales revenues by using demographic information to focus on a particular segment of the population. As an example, a firm may choose to focus on the age of people in a particular market. Age can be broken down into toddler age, pre-school age, school age, teenage years, youth (18–25), adults (25–39), middle age (40–59), and seniors (age 60 plus). Each of these age groups can become a target market for a firm. Examples of retail stores that use demographics to target a particular segment of the market are Gap, Old Navy, Guess, Jacob, Lasenza, Next, Zara, Kiddie Cobbler, and Sports Check. Market segmentation refers to the division of an entire market into smaller market segments that have common characteristics. Instead of selling to the entire market, a firm may choose to sell to only one or a few of the market segments. What are the demographic trends in your firm's industry? How is your firm responding to the trends?

Government Actions

Government actions affect firms in many ways. As a result, a firm needs to monitor the actions of the government and consider them when performing strategic analysis to develop a business strategy. Government actions can create opportunities for firms in some situations. In other instances, government actions can pose a threat to firms. Exhibit 2 shows examples of government actions.

Exhibit 2: Example of government actions

- taxes
- price controls
- subsidies
- product labeling
- minimum wages
- international trade agreements

Each of the above actions can have implications for a firm. For example, the cost of implementing minimum wages will affect a firm's profits. An assessment of costs and benefits is required. Similarly, an increase or decrease in taxes affects the bottom line of a firm. Is any particular government action helping or hurting your firm? How is your firm responding to these government actions?

Ecological (Environmental) Factors

Ecological or environmental factors can have tremendous impact on firms because of their social, health, and monetary cost implications. For example, asthma is on the rise, cancer continues to be a health threat, and pollution is on the mind of every citizen. Smog, soot, haze, and pollution cause diseases such as asthma and cancer. Furthermore, they cause destruction of rivers, lakes, trees, and wildlife. Environmental groups have called on governments to develop laws or policies to limit firms from polluting the environment. Due to the seriousness of the effects of pollution, firms have to be vigilant and proactive in responding to environmental and ecological issues and trends.

Chapter 3

Industry Environment

Firms face many challenges in their industry environment that affect their ability to earn above-average returns. The challenges dim their chances of ever achieving higher growth, higher profitability, or greater market share. Yet some firms are able to stand up to the challenges and achieve success. Why are the average profits of some industries higher? Why do some industries become more attractive than other industries?

This chapter will uncover some of the many challenges firms face in their industry environment. It will show how to increase a firm's understanding of its industry environment in an organized manner so that it can develop an effective strategy to counter the challenges and achieve higher profits, higher market share, or above-average returns.

Profitable Industry Environment (PIE) Model

This model identifies factors in the industry environment that affect the ability of a firm or an industry to earn above-normal profits. The environments in which industries operate differ and as a result, the average profits of firms differ significantly among industries. There are several factors shown in Figure 3 that can significantly affect a firm's profitability. These include:

- Fierce competition among rival firms
- New and potential entrants
- Supplier behaviour
- Buyer behaviour
- Substitute products or services
- Complementary products or services
- Business scandals
- Government action
- Natural disasters

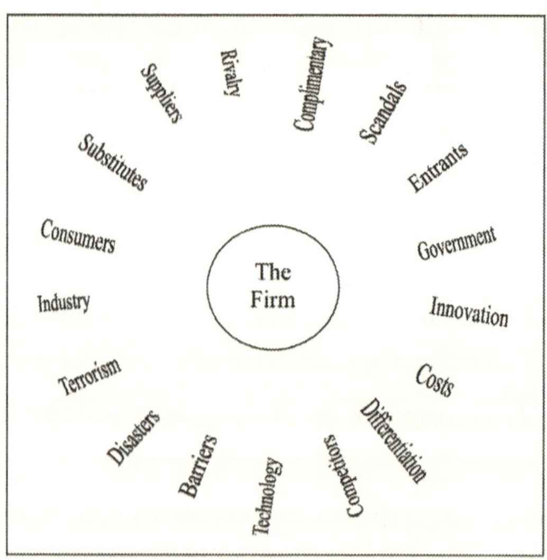

Figure 3: The PIE Model

The impact of these factors can explain differences in earnings among industries. Since the 1980s, only five factors within an industry have been identified as determining a firm's profitability. The factors were (and still are) popularly known as Porter's five forces. Porter used the five forces model to explain the differences in average performance among industries, including why some industries are more attractive than others are. According to Porter's five forces, industries achieve better than average or worse than average profits depending on the extent of the impact of the five forces. However, things have changed since the 1980s. The environment in which businesses operate is not the same. The PIE model is a closer reflection of modern times and, more importantly, complements Porter's five forces.

The Industry Profitability Map (IPM) flows from the PIE. Figure 4 illustrates how to develop an IPM. The IPM is a visual representation of the extent to which each of the PIE factors affects a firm's profitability. The vertical axis represents the components of the PIE, while the level of impact for each PIE factor is on the horizontal axis.

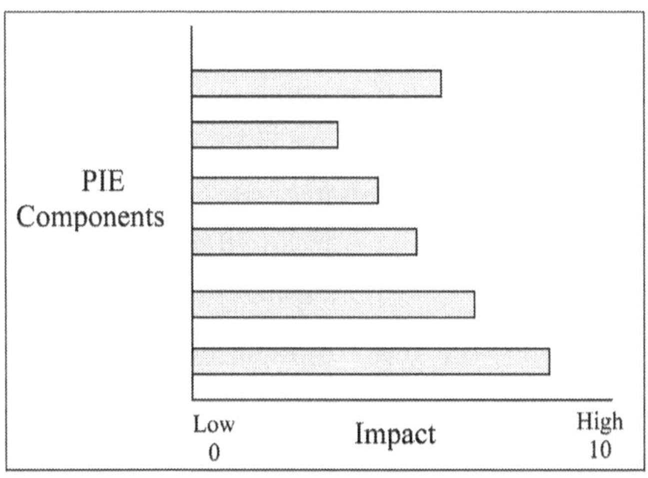

Figure 4: Industry Profitability Map (IPM)

Follow the following four simple steps to develop the IPM:

1. Determine initially what the IPM is being developed for—a firm or an industry as a whole.
2. Consider each PIE factor and determine if it has a lesser or greater impact on the industry as a whole or the firm.
3. Use a scale between zero (no impact) and ten (high impact) to measure the level of impact of each PIE factor.
4. Indicate the level of impact of each component of PIE and develop a graph as shown in Figure 4.

A discussion of some of the PIE factors follows next.

Fierce Competition

Fierce competition among firms in an industry occurs through the intensity of rivalry among firms. Head-to-head competition can threaten profitability of firms within an industry. Intense rivalry occurs especially among firms in markets where firms use different kinds of marketing techniques or competitive moves in an attempt to gain a greater share of the market or simply differentiate their product or services from those of their competitors.

The kinds of competitive moves or marketing techniques firms generally engage in result in reduction in overall performance. Rivalry among firms usually results in price reductions or discounts, high levels of advertising and promotion, as well as warranties and guarantees. All of these competitive moves have the potential to reduce the wealth creation within the industry. As an example, in the airline industry where a high degree of rivalry exists, competitive actions and reactions usually result in competing airlines swiftly matching discount prices of other competing airline carriers. While this is good for consumers, intense rivalry has the potential to reduce profits when firms engage in price discounts and counter price reductions.

Industries where competitors engage in fierce competition include automobile, computer, and soft drink industries. The level of rivalry intensifies when there is a large number of competing firms in a specific industry. Where there is very little product differentiation among competing products, such as with shampoo or toothpaste, competitive rivalry among firms that make the same or similar products increases greatly. The costs of entering or leaving an industry where many firms make the same or similar products are generally lower. Similarly, within such industries, competing firms are usually price takers as they operate in perfect competition market industry. Types of markets such as perfect competition, monopolistic, oligopoly, and monopoly will be discussed later in this chapter.

New and Potential Competitors

New and potential competitors can diminish the average profitability of an industry. New competitors are firms that have recently entered a specific industry. Potential competitors are those who plan to enter and compete in a specific industry. Examples of new competitors include those in automobile and computer industries. New competitors to the North American automobile industry include Toyota, Nissan, Hyundai Motor Corporation, KIA Motors, Mercedes, and BMW. For years General Motors, Ford, Chevrolet, and Chrysler dominated the North American automobile industry. The entry of foreign automobile competitors has posed a serious competitive threat to the North American automobile industry. Similarly, for years, IBM dominated the computer industry. Now there are new entrants such as Hewlett-Packard, Dell, Gateway, Compaq, and others who have claimed their share of the computer market.

There is no doubt that new or potential competitors threaten the profitability of an industry and the performance of firms within the industry. New or potential competitors enter a particular industry when existing firms are earning above-normal profits. Their motivation is to get their piece of the pie. Their entry into the industry can generate a high degree of competitive rivalry, which in turn can result in low-average returns for firms within the industry in the form of lower profits.

Suppliers

Suppliers exercise their power in many ways. They can increase price, reduce quality, restrict supply, or refuse to supply their goods or services. Any of these actions or behaviours on the part of the supplier can threaten the performance, profitability, and in some instances the viability of a firm or an industry.

Firms face the threat of supplier behaviour every day. Firms depend on suppliers for raw materials to produce their products, just as they depend on workers to supply their labour. They depend on bankers and investors to supply them with capital. Any of these suppliers can pose a threat to an industry or firms within the industry.

There are certain characteristics of suppliers that serve as warning signs to indicate that a supplier might be in a position to exercise its power in its dealing with a firm. These warning signs include those shown in Exhibit 3.

Exhibit 3: Warning signs of supplier power

- supplier does not value the business of its clients or customers
- one or few suppliers in the market
- absence of close substitute products or services
- supplier's products or services are difficult to obtain or rare
- switching cost of supplier's products or services is astronomical
- supplier can easily raise prices
- supplier can restrict outputs
- supplier threatens or refuse to supply

Recognizing these behaviours early can minimize the possibility of the supplier squeezing profits out of a firm. Suppliers exercise their power by raising their prices, by limiting the quantity sold to customers, or by simply refusing to deal with a particular customer. The owner of the only gas station located in a remote or small community can exercise supplier power to ration the sale of its gas to farmers so that it can raise the price of the gas and make more money. In exercising its supplier power, the owner of the gas station is able to squeeze the profits out of the farmers in the small community.

Buyers

Concern over the threat of buyer power can be serious enough to warrant investigation by government agencies. This is because the threat of buyer power can threaten profitability of industries and firms within them. For example, buyer power happens when a firm or a group of firms is in a dominant position to negotiate with suppliers and obtain more favourable terms than those obtained by smaller or non-dominant buyers. This can put the dominant firm or group of firms in a stronger competitive position than smaller or non-dominant firms and can restrict competition. Economists refer to this kind of behaviour as a buyer power or monopsony power. A monopsonist is a firm that has a very large share of a market and is able to negotiate very favourable terms, including prices, with suppliers. While a monopoly is a single supplier, a monopsonist is a single buyer.

Monopsonists and their exercise of monopsony power appear in every country. A monopsonist's ability to obtain favourable terms is of particular concern to many advanced economies such as the EU, Canada, and the United States. An example of this concern was the exercise of monopsony power of the supermarket industry over suppliers in the industry. In Europe, the concern was over excessive buyer power and the growth in the concentration of retail firms. This concern was the focus of attention of the European Commission's investigation into the merger of supermarket chains involving Carrefour and Promodes.

Substitutes

Substitutes are products or services that meet the needs of customers in the same way as existing products or services. For example, there are many different ways to travel in any country. One can travel by foot, boat, train, car, airplane, bus, or by motorbike. These are substitutes in the transportation industry. Similarly, VHS players and DVD players are close substitutes; so are national postal services, electronic mail (e-mail), and private courier services. The threat of substitutes and their impact is widely known in economics. Substitutes affect the demand for a product in a negative way and can result in the reduction of profits a firm makes. Are there close substitutes to the products and services your firm offers?

Complementary Products

One way to illustrate complementary products is to use the Parker fountain pen as an example. Before the introduction of Bic ballpoint pens, Parker fountain pens were by far the most popular writing instrument in the market at the time. Parker fountain pens could not have survived on their own without suppliers of ink. The ink complemented Parker pens, since without the ink Parker fountain pens could not provide value to consumers. The ink offered value to the consumers when it was used with the Parker fountain pens to write documents by hand. In economic jargon, the Parker fountain pens and the ink were complementary products.

In modern times, there are many examples of complements. For example, tires are complements of vehicles such as cars, tractors, and airplanes. Intel and Microsoft need each other just as Home Depot needs other businesses in its immediate neighbourhood. Intel and Microsoft each make computer products that enhance each other's products. Home Depot needs to draw more customers to their stores than if they were located in isolation far away from shopping districts.

Complementary products or services can affect the amount purchased, or as economists will say, the quantity demanded. A rise in price of complementary products or services can result in a decrease in the amount demanded of the complement. For example, automobile and gas are complementary products. When there is a rise in automobile prices, consumers will purchase fewer cars and as a result, consumption of gas will decline. Conversely, a decline in the price of complementary products or services can result in more of the complements demanded. Thus, prices of complementary products or services can have a negative or positive effect on demand and subsequently on the revenues of a firm.

What products or services are complementary to those your firm offers? What are their potential impacts on your firm's overall profitability?

Business Scandals

Business scandals and corporate recklessness can shatter business confidence, tarnish the image of business leadership, and diminish investors' confidence. Accounting irregularities and unethical behaviour have resulted in value creation nightmares, crushed employment opportunities, and shattered retirement dreams of employees. Enron, WorldCom, Tyco International, and ImClone are a few examples of reported business scandals. Some Enron officials were alleged or accused of a scheme to hide losses from shareholders, commit money-laundering fraud, or develop conspiracy to commit securities fraud. The company's stock, which traded in December 2000 at an all-time high of $84.87, plummeted to below $1.00 by November 28, 2001. Enron filed for bankruptcy on December 2, 2001. Some Enron officials went to jail. In addition, the majority of Enron employees lost their jobs. Many lost a great portion of their retirement savings with Enron.

WorldCom suffered a similar fate. It filed for bankruptcy due to billions of dollars in accounting errors. The justice system also indicted the former chief executive of Tyco International on charges concerning Tyco's finances. Similarly, ImClone's former CEO went to jail for a little over seven years for insider trading — informing family members to dump ImClone's stock just before the U.S. Food and Drug Administration refused to approve ImClone's drug for sale.

These business scandals sent stock prices plummeting. This resulted in a stock market decline worth nearly 8 trillion dollars in 2000. Business scandals such as those involving Enron, WorldCom, Tyco International, and ImClone destroy wealth creation and profitability of firms. Companies involved in scandals go bankrupt, employees lose their jobs, the stock markets plummet, and investors become jittery and lack the confidence to part with their money.

Government Actions

Most books and guides on strategy do not give the impact of government actions much credit, or they completely ignore the actions of the government in the strategy equation.

Yet government actions play a major role in the profitability of businesses.

Does a government subsidy to some aerospace firms and not others in the same industry concern those firms that did not receive any subsidy? Regardless of the answer, the government can influence the bottom line of firms in an industry. Take for example government agencies, such as Health Canada, which approve pharmaceutical products. The decision of Health Canada to approve, not approve, or delay the approval of a drug for commercialization can have a major effect on the hopes and aspirations of a company.

The government also exercises its power on business through government regulations. Generally, firms must comply with the powers of the government, which firms left on their own will otherwise not do willingly. The government regulates many industries, including home construction, bridge construction, and the automobile industry.

Structure-Conduct-Performance (S-C-P) Model

The structure-conduct-performance (S-C-P) model demonstrates how an industry is organized (market structure), how firms within the industry behave or compete (conduct), and then the impact of the market structure and the behaviour of the firms on the level of performance. (An industry consists of firms that perform similar economic activities).

There is a relationship between the structure of an industry, the behaviour of firms in that industry, and the performance of firms within the industry, as shown in Figure 5. If one knows both the structure of an industry and how the competitors within the industry behave or compete, one can predict whether the firms in that industry will earn normal, above-normal, or below-normal profits. The structure-conduct-performance dynamics in Figure 5 show the main elements of the S-C-P model.

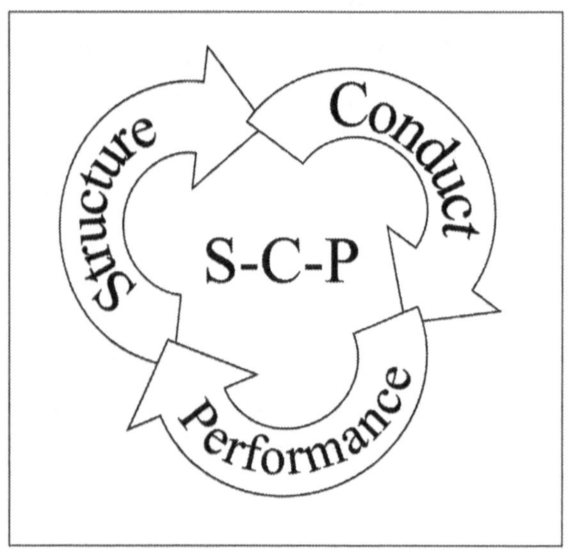

Figure 5: The Structure-Conduct-Performance (S-C-P) Model

The S in S-C-P refers to structure of an industry, which includes entry costs, exit costs, the number of competitors in the industry, and whether the products in that industry are similar or different.

The C refers to the conduct of firms (competitors) within a specific industry; that is, the behaviour of the firms as revealed through product differentiation, marketing, cost leadership, or market power. In this sense, conduct refers to the business strategies firms pursue.

The P refers to the performance of firms within the industry or to the performance of the industry as a whole. The structure of industry determines the conduct or behaviour of firms within it. This in turn determines the profitability of the industry. The S-C-P framework is as shown in Figure 6.

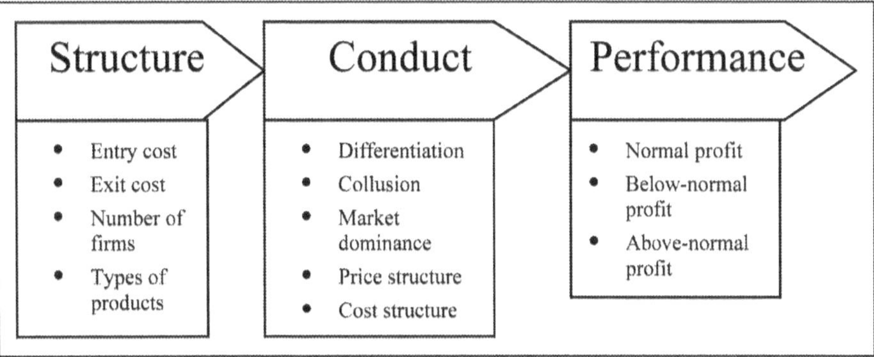

Figure 6: The S-C-P Framework

Exhibit 4 shows examples of questions to consider prior to entering a new market or industry.

Exhibit 4: S-C-P Market entry test questions		
Structure	**Conduct**	**Performance**
• Are there many competitors in the industry?	• Is it costly to enter the industry?	• Do the firms make normal profits?
• Are there only a few firms in the industry?	• Is it costly to leave (exit) the industry?	• Do the firms make above-normal profits?
• Is there a dominant firm?	• Are the firms price takers?	• Do the firms make below-normal profits?

• Is there a differentiation in the products and services? • Is the industry highly regulated by the government?	• Can the firms differentiate their products or services? • Is there a high degree of rivalry among firms?	• What is the market share of the largest competitor? • What is the average return of the industry?

Questions such as those found in Exhibit 4 are useful in understanding industry competitive dynamics.

Industry Structure or Types of Markets

There are four major types of markets.

- Perfect competition
- Monopolistic
- Oligopoly
- Monopoly

Insight into a firm's industry is important in developing a business strategy. When a firm knows the industry in which it operates, it is able to determine which behaviour is feasible in order to earn above-normal profits.

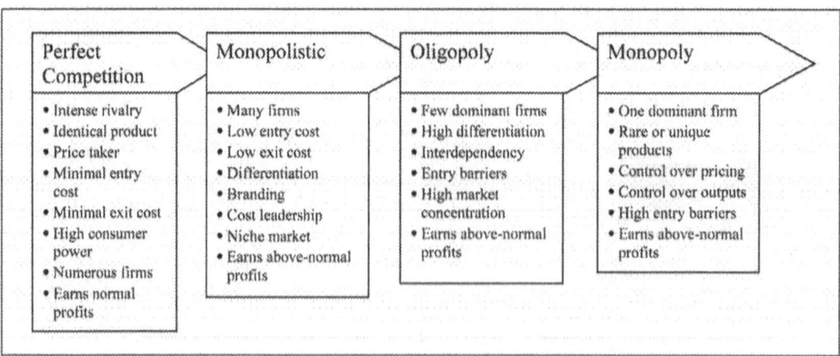

Figure 7: Industry-Market-Structure (IMS)

Ideally, a firm should aim at moving from the left to right, as shown in Figure 7. In other words, a firm would be better off moving from a perfect competition market to a monopolistic market, or from a monopolistic market to an oligopoly, or from an oligopoly to a monopoly. As a firm moves from left to right, its chances of higher overall performance increase. This is because in perfect competition markets, firms generally make normal profits, while firms in a monopolistic market, an oligopoly, or a monopoly generally make above-normal profits.

Consider the following challenge questions:

- How can a firm in perfect competition market move into a lucrative monopolistic market?
- How can a monopolistic firm become a monopoly?
- How does a monopoly firm exercise its market power to make above-normal profits?

You will find answers to these questions in this book as you read on.

Perfect Competition

In a perfect competition industry there are many firms competing with each other for the same customers. The firms in a perfect competition industry sell the same or identical products. Each firm's products or services are indistinguishable from those of the competitors. It is challenging, especially for a single firm, to differentiate its products or services from those of other firms. In this industry, firms are price takers, since no single firm is able to influence prices of products and services. If a firm attempts to charge prices higher than competitors' prices for identical products or services, customers would avoid the firm and buy from its competitors. Examples of businesses that operate in a perfect competition industry include firms, which sell vegetable produce such as corn, or lettuce, hairdressing, and fast food restaurants that sell identical foods such as sandwiches, french-fries and hamburgers. Perfect competition assumes that consumers have perfect information about prices and quality of products each firm offers.

Entry or exist costs for perfect competition industries are minimal. Barriers of entry are virtually non-existent. This makes it easier for potential firms to enter the industry. Competitive rivalry is intense, with each firm trying to survive or make ends meet. Consumers in this industry have a tremendous amount of bargaining power as they enjoy huge availability of similar products and services. Each firm in this industry only commands a tiny market share. The net result is that these firms only earn normal profits. In economic jargon, firms in a perfect competition industry produce and sell at a point where their marginal revenue equals their marginal cost.

Monopolistic

A monopolistic industry consists of many firms competing against one another just as in a perfect competition. The cost to enter and exit such an industry is low. However, firms in a monopolistic industry can earn above-normal profits. This is possible because a monopolistic firm is able to carve out a market niche and differentiate its products and services through branding, advertising, promotion, and packaging. Furthermore, a monopolistic firm is able to reduce its total cost compared to its competitors. It can pass the cost reductions on to its customers in the form of lower prices. Consequently, a monopolistic firm is not a price taker. It can set prices that are different from its competitors and influence the conduct of other competitors. This allows firms in a monopolistic industry to engage in cost leadership and product differentiation. Examples of monopolistic industries are automobile and beer manufacturing industries. Promotion and advertising are common marketing techniques firms use in these industries.

Oligopoly

In an oligopoly industry, there are only few large firms. Typically, the number of firms in this industry is between two to eight dominant firms. Firms in an oligopoly industry produce or sell similar or differentiated products or services.

It is usually costly to enter or exit such an industry. In this industry, firms generally enjoy above-normal performance. However, firms in an oligopoly industry are typically difficult or challenging to manage for higher profits, because each firm has to be vigilant about the actions and reactions of their competitors. Firms in an oligopoly industry are interdependent as to their decisions about pricing and how much to produce or offer for sale to customers.

For example, consider two firms that are oligopoly firms. Both firms charge the same prices for the products they sell to their customers. Both firms sell just about the same quantity of products to the customers. In this scenario, they both generate the same amount of revenues and have equal share of the market. One of the firms decides unilaterally to raise its prices in order to increase its revenues. Customers realize that they can now buy the same products cheaper from the firm that did not raise its prices. Customers rush to this firm to buy their products.

What happens to the firm that raised its prices? That firm would lose revenues and market share to the firm that did not raise its prices. Economists believe that firms in an oligopoly industry are interdependent when it comes to their decisions about pricing and quantity they offer for sale to customers. Interdependence between firms means that each firm considers the likely reactions of other firms and customers within the industry before making decisions about pricing, output, and investments. This is because the action of one firm in an oligopoly industry affects other firms in the industry. This is clearly the case with firms in the airline industry.

There is a tendency for firms in an oligopoly industry to cheat or cooperate on pricing and output decisions. However, oligopolies would rather cooperate than cheat and engage in price wars and production (output) wars. This is because firms within an oligopoly are generally better off if they cooperate rather than compete on prices and outputs. However, because each firm makes its own pricing and output decisions, trust and cooperation among firms are major challenges to firms in this industry. For these reasons, firms in an oligopoly industry are caught in a dilemma that is generally referred to as prisoner's dilemma.

Monopoly

A monopoly industry is the opposite of a perfect competition industry. One firm dominates a monopoly industry. Since a monopolist has no other competitors, it can set any price for its products and services as high as the market can bear. Generally, firms in monopoly industries earn above-normal profits because of their ability to exercise their monopoly power to restrict supply and raise prices.

A monopoly firm usually has unique or rare products and services to offer its customers. Monopoly industries put up high entry barriers in order to keep away potential competitors. Entry barriers can range from high entry cost to resources and capabilities required to enter and remain in the monopoly industry. Examples of firms that dominated their industry at one time were Polaroid in the instant photography industry and Microsoft in the personal computer operating systems market.

Direct Competitor Map (DCM)

Firms or organizations differ in their resources and levels of skills in such areas as marketing, research and development, and innovation. Furthermore, not all firms enjoy the same economies of scale, economies of scope, cost advantages, and other capabilities. Economies of scale come about when a firm's costs decline as its output increases. Diseconomies of scale occur when a firm's costs increase as its output increases. Economies of scope occur when the cost of producing two products together is lesser than producing the two products separately.

The way firms conduct themselves or the actions they take in the marketplace (and how consumers perceive them) reveal a lot about the kind of business strategy they are pursuing. For example, a firm that is pursuing cost leadership strategy is able to offer its customers much lower prices than competitors in the same market segment. Similarly, a firm may pursue a differentiation strategy that gives it an image that distinguishes it from its competitors in the consumers' eyes.

Firms also compete on different dimensions such as price, differentiation, quality, service, warranties, or guarantees. Firms that offer similar products or services and use similar strategy are direct competitors. Direct competitors pursue the same or similar strategies. They compete on dimensions such as price, quality, product, and so on, within the market segment they serve. Figure 8 shows examples of imaginary firms that follow similar business strategies in a particular target market segment.

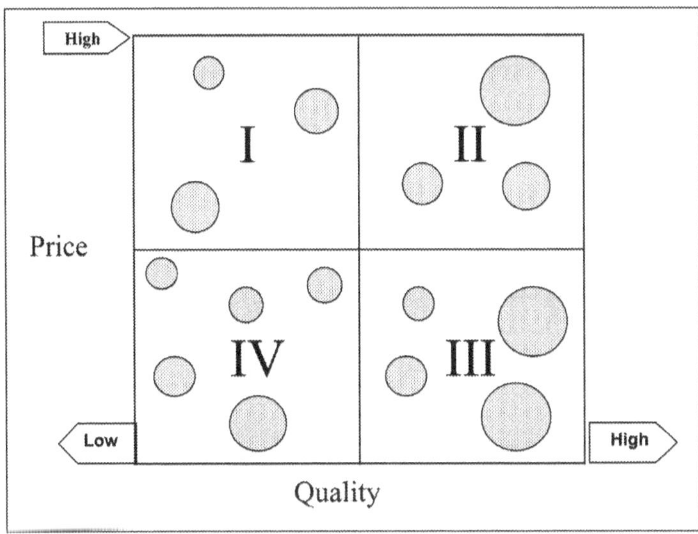

Figure 8: Direct Competitor Map (DCM)

A direct competitor map (DCM) has four market segments. Each quadrant consists of major competitors who pursue the same competitive strategy or a similar one. The assumption for the DCM is that the firms compete only on two dimensions such as price and quality. Firms in the lower left quadrant (IV) compete on lowest price and lowest product quality. At the opposite extreme, firms located in the upper right quadrant (II) compete on high price and high quality. Interpret the rest of the DCM in the same way. With this information, a firm is able to identify which market segment it wants to be in, or which competitors it is up against in a particular market segment.

The DCM allows a firm to focus on its business strategy in relation to the business strategies of its direct competitors. It forces a firm to focus on these important questions:

- Who are your firm's direct competitors?
- What business strategies do these competitors use?
- What business strategy does your firm need to dominate its market?
- Is your current business strategy working for your firm?
- How did your firm decide on the current business strategy?

Business Intelligence (BI)

Competitors are always ready to snatch customers from each other. At the least opportune moment, competitors will not hesitate to get the lion's share of the market. However, a firm that takes the time to understand its environment and competitors is better able to respond to competitive threats and opportunities. One critical and necessary activity that a firm must undertake to respond to threats, opportunities, and competitors, is to gather and analyze business intelligence. This activity is not a one-time thing; firms must include business intelligence as part of their business functions.

When gathering business intelligence, you are trying to understand the firms against whom you are competing. How they behave in the marketplace. What are their goals, strategies, mission, vision, resources, and capabilities?

Firms respond differently when faced with competitive threats or opportunities. Competitive threats and opportunities take many forms, such as attacking an incumbent's market share and seizing the opportunity to grab a much greater market share, or focusing on a niche market. The net effect is to redistribute the total market share or the revenues generated from the entire market.

How a firm behaves in the marketplace depends on many factors; such as future goals, strategic intent, assumptions, current strategy, resources and capabilities, core competence, management competence, and management beliefs.

Future goals of a company can include, but are not limited to, business unit goals, business portfolio goals, strategic positioning goals and corporate parent goals, recruitment and retention goals, marketing goals, sales target goals, plant location goals, market target goals, and innovation goals.

Many firms have an overall corporate goal. However, business unit levels and functional unit levels within a firm should each have their own goals. For example, the goals of a marketing division and manufacturing division will be different from one another, even though they are within the same firm. Corporate goals and business unit goals provide a source of valuable information in understanding threats and opportunities in the business environment.

Assumptions firms make tell much about their business strategy. Management preferences, especially personal beliefs, play a major role in strategy actions and strategic direction of a firm. For example, managers who have a strong desire for power and need for achievement will more likely be attracted to high-risk projects. On the other hand, managers who seek security will be more cautious in responding to competitive challenges.

Equally important is the knowledge of competitors' current strategy, resources, and capabilities. This provides additional knowledge and understanding of competitive risks and opportunities. A solid analysis can help determine appropriate response to threats and opportunities.

Business Intelligence Sources (BIS)

Information is everywhere. Firms can collect business intelligence from many sources. There are two main sources of business intelligence: primary sources and secondary sources. The primary sources of business intelligence include face-to-face surveys and telephone surveys. Secondary sources of business intelligence include data from a company's internal records and from external sources. External data sources consist of open source intelligence (OSI) and classified source intelligence (CSI). Generally, government agencies and organizations hold confidential or secret information that is classified source intelligence (CSI). They also routinely collect and publish information for public consumption.

Collecting intelligence about a competitor's future goals, assumptions, current strategy, resources and capabilities, core competence, and management competence can be time consuming and sometimes quite challenging. Nevertheless, other competitors are committed to business intelligence. Law enforcement and military communities use OSI extensively. There is no doubt that businesses, competitors, and business executives can benefit from OSI. This intelligence can be obtained ethically and legally from non-classified public information sources.

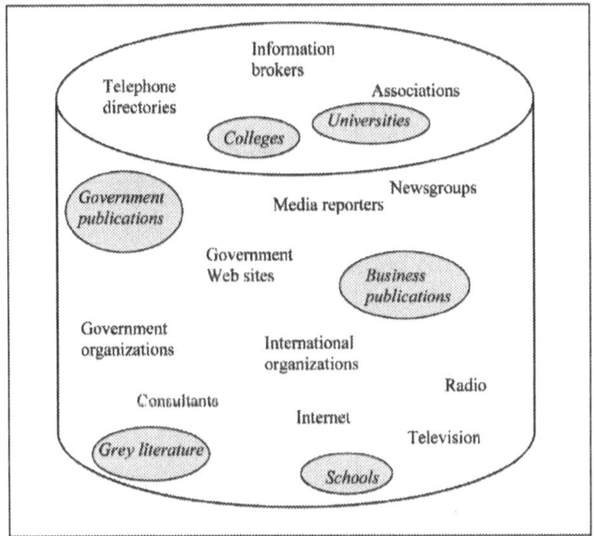

Figure 9: Open Source Intelligence (OSI)

OSI includes, but is not limited to, information from the following sources:

- Conversations with government officials
- Companies
- Financial and investment communities
- Drive-by observations

- Colleges or universities
- Libraries
- Information brokers
- Grey literature
- Government institutions
- Government publications

Figure 9 shows examples of business intelligence sources. Government institutions, for example, routinely collect information about industries that they publish for public consumption. Conversations with appropriate government officials can reveal a lot about what is happening in a specific industry and in the labour market.

Grey literature can be an excellent source of business intelligence. This information is produced on a non-commercial basis, and is generally free. Examples of grey literature are internal newsletters, and some government publications.

The profile of a firm's management team can also reveal the nature of decisions the firm would make, and the actions it would take under certain circumstances. For example, the universities and colleges attended by the members of a firm's management team can be a great source of intelligence. Some universities and colleges have a conservative orientation, while others have a liberal orientation. Such information can be helpful, for example, in assessing whether firms and their leaders would be compatible with each other in an alliance or merger situations.

Lenders can confirm the existence of a firm (borrower) by using drive-by observation before they advance loans to a borrower. A firm that has several store locations can use drive-by observation to determine the peak periods and volume of customers to a particular store location.

In this age of information and knowledge-based economies, the amount of information sources can be endless. Regarding business intelligence on the international market, there are many sources from which to choose. For example, Canada has the Statistics Canada Catalogue, Canadiana, and Canadian Periodical Index. Britain publishes an Annual Abstract of Statistics. The U.S. government produces many publications to assist businesses.

Private sources that provide intelligence on business trends include:

- Frost and Sullivan (http://www.frost.com/)
- Euromonitor (http://www.euromonitor.com/)
- Economist Intelligence Unit (http://www.eiu.com/)

Numerous business intelligence sources are available today, thanks to the Internet. Intelligence gathering takes time and is like putting together a jigsaw puzzle. It is accomplished one piece at a time with each piece contributing to the overall results one-step at a time.

Business Intelligence Framework (BIF)

Following the framework in Figure 10 for conducting business intelligence is similar to conducting research. The first step is to establish the purpose of the business intelligence. The purpose should clearly define the business intelligence problem in terms of what the information would be used for, who would use it, and when the intelligence would be used. The second step is to define clearly the question that the business intelligence will answer and the scope of the business intelligence. For example, a question might be why does our firm's market share keep declining? The scope of the business intelligence may include finding out more about current and potential competitors.

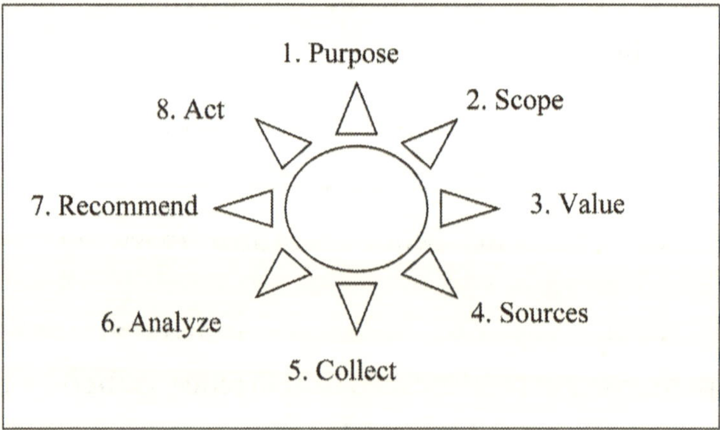

Figure 10: Business Intelligence Framework (BIF)

The third step is to determine the value of the business intelligence. This means comparing the anticipated benefits of the business intelligence with the anticipated cost of gathering the intelligence. In addition, consider the cost to the firm for not collecting business intelligence. The fourth step is to identify the sources of business intelligence as discussed earlier. The sources should include open source intelligence. The fifth step is to collect information from the business intelligence sources. Since there are numerous sources nowadays where business intelligence can be collected, a firm must be selective and evaluate the business intelligence sources. It is important to note that there can be misinformation as well, designed to mislead competitors. The sixth step is to analyze the information. The seventh step is to prepare recommendations for the intended user. The last step is to act on the business intelligence as soon as possible, since the information can become outdated.

Chapter 4

Internal Environment

The internal environment presents opportunities as well as challenges to a firm. This chapter introduces several business frameworks and models aimed at uncovering a firm's internal strengths, weaknesses, opportunities, and threats. The frameworks and models include:

- SWOT
- Market segmentation
- PVCS
- Market share analysis
- Relative market share
- Resources and capabilities
- ARC framework
- Business blind spots
- Competitive advantage

These form part of the knowledge and understanding required for developing a strategy mindset for achieving better and faster results.

SWOT

SWOT stands for strengths, weaknesses, opportunities, and threats, as shown in Figure 11.

A firm can use SWOT to understand its internal and external environments and gain better insights into its capabilities to compete successfully. The ability to capitalize on strengths, eliminate weaknesses, exploit opportunities, and neutralize threats is required to earn above-average profits, or to achieve higher market share or growth. To succeed in the competitive world, a firm must eliminate or minimize weaknesses and threats. It must capitalize on its strengths and exploit opportunities.

Sun Tzu, a Chinese military strategist, pointed out in 500 B.C. that knowing one's self as well as knowing a lot about the enemy one will face could assure victory in every battle. On the other hand, Sun Tzu warned that defeat in battle is always certain when one is ignorant of the enemy and ignorant of one's self. Sun Tzu's observations about military strategy are as applicable today in business as they were for his army in 500 B.C.

The competitive arena is a war zone. Competitors who want to get the greatest share of the market will do almost anything to woo customers away from other firms. This is evident in various marketing techniques that firms use such as advertising, promotion, packaging, pricing, improved products, and customer service. In order to achieve the desired results, a firm must not only know its customers, but must know its strengths and weaknesses, as well as the strengths and weaknesses of its major competitors. A firm must perform a SWOT assessment on itself and on its competitors and then make decisions about them in order to have a reasonable chance of winning competitive battles.

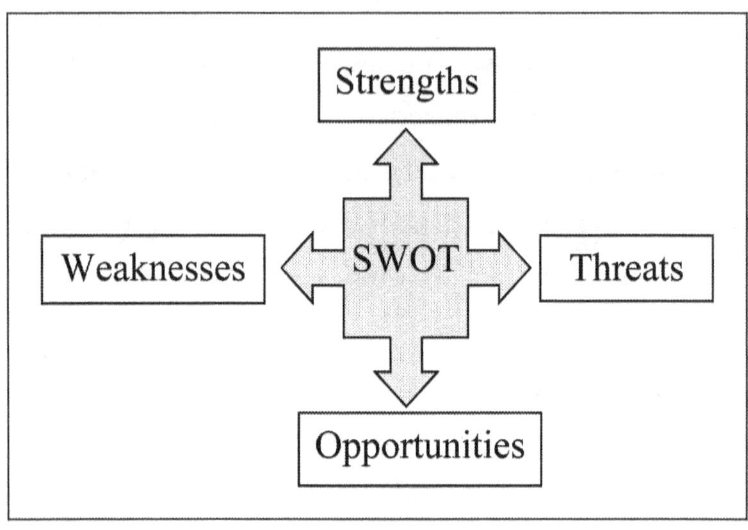

Figure 11: SWOT Model

The SWOT model provides a structured approach to identify factors that affect a firm. It uncovers areas in which a firm excels, where it is most vulnerable, opportunities it can capitalize on, and the negative factors that pose a threat. In order to successfully compete and improve performance, a firm must be able to match its strengths with its weaknesses, and opportunities with threats in its environment. SWOT is a self-discovery framework, which helps explore the business environment and provides greater self-awareness to decision-makers.

Firms can use the SWOT to profile a competitor as well. A SWOT profile is a summary of a firm's strengths, weaknesses, opportunities, and threats at a glance. In providing a snapshot, it creates an awareness of the environment landscape within which the firm operates.

How to Develop a SWOT Profile

There is no single way to develop a SWOT profile. A firm can develop a SWOT profile in a group or individual setting. A group setting involves a brainstorming session, which requires a facilitator. An alternative to a brainstorming session is to allow individuals to provide feedback separately on the firm's strengths, weaknesses, opportunities, and threats.

Follow these three simple steps to develop a SWOT profile.

1. List all the major activities that the firm performs. (For example, see the left column of Exhibit 5).
2. Take each activity and assess its impact on the firm—strengths, weaknesses, opportunities, and threats.
3. Indicate the action to take to eliminate or minimize threats and weaknesses, and exploit opportunities and strengths for each activity. (Refer to the last column of Exhibit 5).

Exhibit 5: A firm's SWOT profile

Activities	Strengths	Weaknesses	Opportunities	Threats	Impact on firm	What to do
Product						
Price						
Advertising						
Marketing program						
Promotion						
Distribution						
Sales						
Purchasing						
Inventory management						
Production						
Manufacturing						
Warehousing						

Dealer support						
Customer service						
Location						
Organization						
Technology						
Research and development						
Innovation						
Planning						
Financing and control						
Management and leadership						
Resources						
Capabilities						
Human resources management						

For example, take the firm's activity in innovation. The firm should indicate whether it is strong on innovation or weak on innovation, and whether it is fully exploiting opportunities with its innovation capability. What threat does the firm face for not taking advantage of opportunities? What is the impact of the strengths, weaknesses, opportunities, and threats on the firm's ability to compete successfully and improve the bottom line? What course of action should be taken on these matters?

Production Value Chain System (PVCS)

A firm is a production system engaging in activities that aim at providing value to consumers. The idea behind the Production Value Chain System (PVCS) is that products or services go through various stages. Other activities support the various stages of production before they finally reach consumers. Each stage in the production system adds value to consumers, hence the name Production Value Chain System. The PVCS uses the input-process-output production system shown in Figure 12. Each activity depends on the completion of previous activities in the production chain and contributes to the final product or service before it reaches the consumer. Each activity must add value to the consumer.

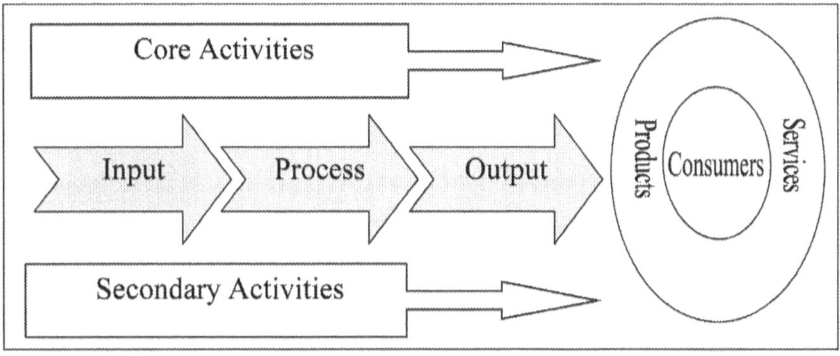

Figure 12: Production Value Chain System (PVCS)

The stages in the production system consume money, which affect the firm's other resources, such as financial resources, human resources, technology, and physical resources. Since each production activity consumes resources, a firm must assess each activity and how it adds value to customers. A firm is better off eliminating activities that consume plenty of resources and add very little value to the customer. On the other hand, a firm should encourage activities that add value to the ultimate consumer. When the value created for the customer exceeds the cost of creating the value, the firm earns profits. On the other hand, if the cost of creating value to the consumer exceeds revenues from the product, a firm will earn below-normal profits. For example, DVD players in minivans keep kids entertained while parents drive. To make this added feature profitable to the firm, the value to the consumer must exceed the cost of this innovation. If the sale of minivans increases because of this added feature

(DVD), then everything being equal, this will result in higher revenues and profits for the firm.

The importance of the PVCS in business strategy is that it forces a firm to look at its activities and assess costs relative to the value they bring to their customers. This can result in a decision to continue performing certain activities, stop performing certain activities, or improve the performance of certain activities. These kinds of internal self-assessments can help a firm focus on activities that are important to its ultimate consumer. A firm must avoid activities that waste resources and add little or no value to its customers.

The PVCS provides a framework for a firm to group its activities into core business activities and secondary activities. Core business activities are those that are directly traceable to the ultimate consumer. These are generally the reason why the business exists. Core activities vary from firm to firm. Examples of core business activities for a manufacturing firm are the processing of raw materials into finished products. Secondary activities are those that are not the focus of a firm but are necessary for the firm to carry out the core business activities of the firm. Examples of secondary activities can include marketing, sales, distribution, advertising, human resources management, technology infrastructure, finance and administration, legal, and so on. The PVCS differs from one firm to the next. There is no one PVCS for all firms. The PVCS of one firm can be entirely different from that of another firm down the road.

Use the questions in Exhibit 6 to determine whether your firm's core activities and secondary activities add value to the consumer. Which activities should your firm start doing, continue doing, or stop doing?

Exhibit 6: Production value chain questions

Core activities

- Do the activities add value to the ultimate consumer?
- How much do the activities cost?
- Which activities should the firm continue doing?
- Which activities should the firm stop doing?
- Which activities must the firm improve on?

Secondary activities

- Do the activities add value to the ultimate consumer?
- How much do the activities cost?
- Which activities should the firm continue doing?
- Which activities should the firm stop doing?
- Which activities must the firm improve on?

Market Segmentation (MS)

Market segmentation (MS) breaks the entire market into several smaller groups of markets called market segments or target markets. MS sorts out consumers into groups and creates a market segment with common characteristics or variables that make it easier to identify customers in each market segment.

Exhibit 7: Segmentation variables			
Demographic	**Geographic**	**Psychographic**	**Consumption**
• income • gender • occupation • family size • home ownership • religion • education • age • ethnic origin • marital status	• population • continent • country • province/state • city/town • urban/suburban • rural • metropolitan • region • climate	• hobbies • activities • interests • lifestyle • opinions • personality • image • social status	• brand loyalty • heavy users • practical users • spendthrift

Exhibit 7 shows examples of variables used for market segmentation. They include demographic, geographic, psychographic, and consumption variables. As Figure 13 shows, the entire market is broken into smaller markets called target markets. The process of grouping consumers into groups with common characteristics is market segmentation.

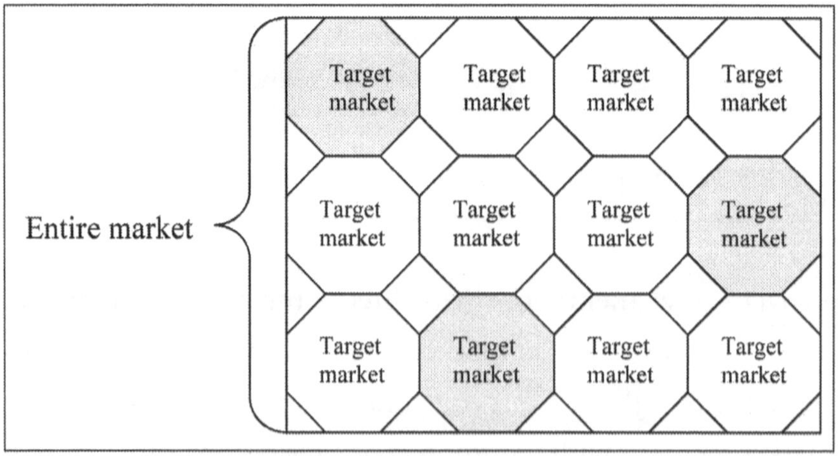

Figure 13: Market segmentation

The grouping into smaller markets of common characteristics allows a firm to focus on a particular market segment called a target market. For example, a firm may choose to offer its products or services to a target market (market segment) consisting of consumers who have incomes ranging from $80,000 to $120,000, live in the province of Ontario in Canada, are twenty-five to thirty-five years old, and are avid golfers. What is your firm's target market? How lucrative is this target market?

Market Share

Market share provides an indication of how well or poorly a firm is doing in the competitive arena. It is one of the commonly used indicators of a firm's performance. There is a relationship between a firm's market share and its performance in a growing market. A firm with 90 percent market share, in an industry that is growing, is definitely performing well.

Exhibit 8 shows how a firm's market share is calculated. Market share represents a percentage that a firm has out of the total market of the industry in which it operates. The total market represents the total units sold or the total monetary value of products or services sold to customers by all the firms in an industry.

Exhibit 8: Percentage market share calculation

Example:

Let us assume that the total dollar value of CDs sold by all firms in Canada is $200 million. One firm sold $180 million. What is the market share of the firm? First, divide $180m by $200m. Multiply the result by 100 to get the percentage market share. The result is a 90 percent market share. The firm's competitors have only 10 percent of the entire market (100 percent minus 90 percent).

If a firm has been in business for two or more years, it can do a trend analysis of its market share performance. Not only does the trend analysis reveal the firm's market share performance over a period compared to the industry, it can also reveal if increases in annual sales revenues translate into better market share performance. Consider the information in Exhibit 9.

Exhibit 9: Market share performance

Year	Firm's annual total sales (million dollars)	Industry's annual total sales (million dollars)	Firm's market share percentage
1	10	**100**	10
2	14	**200**	7
3	18	**300**	6
4	20	**400**	5

The firm's annual total monetary sales have been climbing steadily since Year 1. However, its yearly market share has been declining each year. The annual total sales of the firm doubled from $10 million in Year 1 to $20 million in Year 4. However, the firm's market share actually declined from 10 percent in Year 1 to 5 percent in Year 4. This represents a decline in the firm's market share by 50 percent between Year 1 and Year 4. There could be many possible reasons for the declining market share of the firm. It could be lack of motivation on the part of the sales team or weakness in the firm's distribution, promotion, pricing methods, or the product itself. It could also be that competitors have found a way to innovate. These revelations are important in strategy development. Further investigation may uncover several sources of weakness.

A firm can also use market share to make important decisions about marketing. Consider the example in Exhibit 10, which shows the amounts of beer sold by each firm, and the respective market shares in a specific geographic region, such as the Metro Toronto area. The sale of the beer was in cartons (units) containing twenty-four bottles of beer. Total cartons (units) of beer sold in a year between the firms are 25,000 units.

Exhibit 10: Market share analysis

Names of Firms	Units sold	Unit market share %	Price per carton (unit)	Sales volume ($)	Market share based on sales volume ($)
Firm 1	8,750	35%	$10	$87,500	19.44%
Firm 2	6,250	25%	$20	$125,000	27.78%
Firm 3	5,000	20%	$15	$75,000	16.67%
Firm 4	3,750	15%	$30	$112,500	25.00%
Firm 5	1,250	5%	$40	$50,000	11.11%
Total	25,000	100%		$450,000	100%

A firm can make several important decisions with the information in Exhibit 10. For example, while Firm 1 ranks number one in market share based on units sold, it trails

Firm 2 and Firm 4 in market share in dollar sales volume. What counts as a bottom line is the monetary value of sales and not just the number of units sold.

Each firm has important decisions to make in order to improve their respective market shares based on sales volume. In economics, sales volume is determined by price and quantity sold (demand). The amount that consumers will purchase depends on several factors, such as the availability of substitute products, the price of substitute products, consumer taste, or the incomes of consumers. Firm 5 will have to assess whether its low sales volume is due to an insufficient sales team covering a large market territory; or that consumers are rejecting the beer because the price is much higher than comparable beer in the market. Is it the taste of Firm 5's beer or lack of a motivated sales team or just plain poor marketing? These kinds of questions are critical to improving a firm's performance. What is your firm's market share? What target market share, have you set for your firm?

Relative Market Share (RMS)

It is not sufficient to look at a firm's market share only in relation to its industry. A firm needs to know where it stands in relation to its largest competitor. Relative market share (RMS) compares the market share of a firm to the market share of its largest competitor. Unlike market share, which is in percentages, relative market share is a ratio between the annual total sales of a firm and the annual total sales of its largest competitor. Relative market share is found by dividing the firm's total sales by the total sales of its largest competitor, as shown in Exhibit 11. The resulting figure is in times, for example, two times (2X), three times, four times, and so on. Whether a monetary value of sales or a unit value of sales is used, the interpretation is done in the same manner. Who is your major competitor? What is your firm's relative market share?

Exhibit 11: Relative market share calculation

Example:

Let us assume that the total annual sale of a firm is $90 million. The total annual sale of the firm's largest competitor is $30 million. The relative market share of the firm is 3x (i.e., $90m divided by $30m). This means the firm's relative market share is three times greater than the largest competitor.

Resources and Capabilities

A firm's resources consist of tangible and intangible resources. Tangible resources include buildings, equipment, land, and financial resources. Intangible resources include goodwill, human resources, and intellectual property rights (IPR) such as copyrights, trademarks, and patents. Most organizations take stock of their tangible assets. The balance sheet of a firm's financial statements shows tangible assets. However, the balance sheet or the income statement will not show a firm's capabilities. Capabilities are skills, expertise, and competencies to perform an activity effectively and efficiently. Technology application, management talent, a competent workforce, and innovation are but a few examples of capabilities.

Capabilities are as critical to a firm as the resources it needs to compete. Lack of resources and capabilities can lead to a resource gap or a capability gap. A resource gap is the difference between current resources and the resources required to complete a specific business objective. For example, if a firm currently has $200 million to undertake a marketing program and the firm needs $300 million to launch this marketing program, the firm in this case has a resource gap of $100 million. Similar reasoning applies to a capability gap. A capability gap occurs when current capability falls short of the capability required to complete a strategy objective. For example, if one hundred engineers are needed to complete a technical project and only twenty engineers are currently on hand, there is a capability gap of eighty engineers.

Canada is currently experiencing a shortage of medical doctors. Some families are unable to find medical doctors to provide them with medical care. This is clearly a classic case of a resource and capability gap. Resource and capability gaps affect overall performance results.

The core competence of a firm refers to the skills a firm is able to pull together to perform activities in such a way that they give the firm a competitive advantage. The results achieved through the collective skills become greater than results that individuals working separately can achieve. This is particularly important for firms searching for ways to gain competitive advantage or sustainable competitive advantage. Resources and capabilities must add value to a firm's performance.

Activities, Resources, and Capabilities (ARC)

Firms compete by performing activities with their resources and capabilities. Whether or not the activities, resources, and capabilities permit a firm to gain competitive advantage or sustainable competitive advantage depends on how rare and valuable those resources and capabilities are, and how costly it is to obtain them. Merely possessing resources and capabilities is not sufficient to gain a competitive advantage or to acquire a sustainable competitive advantage. It will depend on the ability of the firm to exploit the resources and capabilities.

A firm has a competitive advantage when it has resources or capabilities that are unmatched by competitors. While there is no standard definition of sustainable competitive advantage, it is generally understood that when a firm continues to enjoy a competitive advantage over an extended period, and this advantage is unmatched by competitors, one can say that the firm enjoys a sustainable competitive advantage.

J.B. Barney developed a VRIO framework as one way of analyzing a firm's internal environment. VRIO stands for value, rarity, inimitability, and organization, and focuses on the firm's resources and capabilities. Prior to Barney's VRIO, firms relied on the SWOT to assess their internal environment. The VRIO assumes that a firm can enjoy a sustainable competitive advantage through its resources and capabilities.

Exhibit 12: ARC framework

Activities, Resources, Capabilities	Value to customers	One of a kind	Costly and hard to copy	Fully exploited	Competitive advantage	Sustainable competitive advantage (SCA)	Adds to or decreases profits
Technology							
Distribution							
Manufacturing							
Human resources management							
Compensation							
Customer service							
Competent employees							
Geographic location							
Marketing							

The ARC framework illustrated in Exhibit 12 goes a step further and complements the VRIO. A firm can focus its internal assessment using the following questions in conjunction with the framework shown in Exhibit 12:

- Do the firm's resources, management capabilities, and innovation add value to customers?
- Are the resources, management capabilities, and innovation one of a kind?
- Are the resources, management capabilities, and innovations costly to develop and hard to copy?
- Is the firm exploiting its resources, management capabilities, and innovation fully?
- Do the resources, management capabilities, and innovation translate into a competitive advantage or a sustainable competitive advantage?
- Do the resources, management capabilities, and innovation increase profits or decrease profits?
- Which activities should the firm continue to perform?
- Which activities should the firm stop performing?
- Which activities must the firm improve?
- Which activities should the firm start performing?

What are your firm's capabilities? What activities contribute to your competitive advantage or sustainable competitive advantage?

Competitive Advantage

A firm can have a competitive advantage, competitive disadvantage, or competitive parity in the marketplace. A firm has a competitive advantage when it has resources, capabilities, or core competencies that no other competitor possesses. These must be hard or costly to imitate. A competitive advantage affects a firm's performance in a positive way. When a firm enjoys a competitive advantage, its net profits or market share can increase. A firm that is at a competitive disadvantage is likely to have below-normal performance.

When is a firm at a competitive disadvantage? Let us take for example two firms that sell the same products. One firm uses a toll-free telephone system and the Internet to take customer orders. In the case of the other firm, customers have to dial in at their own expense to place orders. In this case, the latter firm can be at a disadvantage, while the former can have a competitive advantage. If the firm that uses customer dial-in for order taking continues its practice, it can give the firm that uses modern technology such as the Internet a competitive advantage and possibly a sustainable competitive advantage, if this method of order taking is what consumers prefer.

A firm has competitive parity when it has neither a competitive advantage nor a competitive disadvantage. For example, consider an industry with several competitors that produce the same products with the same types of equipment and raw materials, and there are no differences in the prices of the products. Such firms are in a perfect competition industry. None of the firms has a competitive advantage over the other and none is at a competitive disadvantage. Each firm has competitive parity since they are price takers. Each will earn normal performance or normal profits. What is your firm's competitive advantage? Can the firm sustain the competitive advantage? Has the firm considered innovation?

Business Blind Spots

Business blind spots describe situations when a firm ignores business signals, interprets the signals incorrectly, takes events and economic indicators for granted, or responds to market signals at a slower rate than they should. An example of a business blind spot occurred when Mr. Bill Gates, CEO of Microsoft Corporation, underestimated the commercial necessity of the Internet and failed to understand its commercial potential.

Executives and managers are generally a busy breed of individuals. Some are busy with building capabilities, setting directions, assessing performance, and implementing change. Others occupy their time attending meetings, calling on major customers, drumming up new business, or solving crises. While some firms pay attention to their business environment, others are not particularly attentive to it.

When executives or managers pay little or no attention to market signals and market forces, undetected potential threats occur. Some firms simply choose to ignore market signals even when the realities of the marketplace stare them right in the face. This can happen because of beliefs, policies, or business philosophies that the firm is unwilling to let go. When these have nothing to do with current market realities or the competitive environment, they can result in business blind spots that can threaten the viability of a business.

There are many contributing factors to blind spots of businesses. These include assumptions that organizations hold that are far from market reality, management beliefs and philosophy, corporate policies, and practices that go unchallenged. Gilad, in his book Business Blind Spots, provides examples of how companies became victims of the destructive power of business blind spots. Some examples of firms in Gilad's book that were victims of business blind spots were Sears, Roebuck & Co. and Hoffmann-La Roche.

Business strategy must take into account a firm's blind spots. This means, from time to time, a firm must review its policies, its assumptions, and its management beliefs to see whether they help or hinder the firm's competitive position and whether they are consistent with the firm's vision and mission as well as the direction in which it wants to go.

PART II

Business Strategy Landscape

Chapter 5

The Landscape of Business Strategy

Academics and practitioners do not agree on the definition of strategy. Different kinds of strategy definitions exist in books and articles on business strategy. People use strategy in daily conversations and yet, ask a hundred people and each will have a different perspective on strategy. There is no doubt strategy has different meanings to different people.

Henry Mintzberg described strategy as a plan, a ploy, a pattern, a position, or a perspective. Michael Porter saw business strategy as being about market positioning using differentiation, overall cost leadership, and focus on gaining competitive advantage. For Andrew and Barney, strategy was about gaining competitive advantage or sustainable competitive advantage with resources and capabilities. Prahalad's core competency strategy advocated leveraging learning and competencies to gain competitive advantage. Miles and Snow's observations of firms resulted in their identification of four types of strategy, which firms use to compete. They named the four types of strategy as defenders, reactors, prospectors, and analyzers.

Even if there is no agreement on the definition of strategy, one thing is certain. Every firm exists to make money and seek to increase profitability, growth, market share, or overall performance.

The real issue is not what business strategy is, because there are numerous points of view on business strategy and people continue to add their views to the subject matter. At the core of strategy are the knowledge of strategy, the choice of strategy, and the application of strategy to gain competitive advantage or sustainable competitive advantage. The real issue is about being knowledgeable and smart about strategy, making the right strategy choice, and using strategy effectively to achieve better and faster results.

Firms face constant challenges in their external, internal, and industry environments. With globalization and free markets between countries on the rise, competition has become more intense among local, national, and international companies. Competition among firms continues to increase as foreign firms enter domestic markets. Even within their own borders, firms are constantly searching for innovative ways to expand markets and improve overall profitability. Multinational firms such as MacDonald's, Microsoft, and Wal-Mart constantly look for ways to generate more revenues and improve their overall performance.

Firms make decisions and choices about how they will increase profitability, market share, growth, and overall performance. They decide on the strategy that best responds to their environment to yield the most favourable results. Not only do firms respond to their environment, they can also create an environment to which their competitors must respond. Firms not only must understand threats and weaknesses in their environment, but more importantly, they must select among various strategy choices to neutralize threats, and exploit opportunities and strengths, while simultaneously minimizing weaknesses. The kinds of strategy choices will depend in large measure on the firm's knowledge about the strategy landscape.

One of the objectives of this book is to provide the knowledge and understanding necessary for developing a strategy mindset and a mental map for achieving better and faster results. This chapter coaches the decision-maker systematically towards achieving a higher overall profitability, a higher growth and a greater market share.

Types of Strategy in a Firm

Typically, firms organize themselves around activities they perform. Firms also organize themselves in a hierarchical manner. Within the same organization, there can be many units, branches, or departments. A firm can have an overall strategy and at the same time have several strategies at different levels of the organization. There are three main types of strategy within an organization: corporate strategy, business strategy or business unit strategy, and functional or operational strategy.

Figure 14: Types of Strategy in a Firm

Corporate strategy is about the overall direction of an organization. It is concerned with the mission, vision, the overall health of the organization, the kind of business the firm should be in, and the strategic direction of the firm. Corporate strategy is concerned with broad strategy requiring decisions about the entire firm. For example, decisions about mergers and acquisitions or the kinds of business the firm should be in will require a corporate strategy. Similarly, decisions involving the allocation of resources through corporate budgetary process can fall under corporate strategy. Generally, managers and executives at the highest level of the organization determine corporate strategy.

Business strategy decisions occur at the middle levels of an organization and, of course, with the approval from the top management. Business unit strategy is concerned with how to engage in competition. For example, a business unit will be concerned with resources and capabilities, how to compete, which markets to compete in, what products and services to compete with, what market share to achieve. A business unit has a product-market focus. Figuratively speaking, it is like a firm within a larger firm.

Business units are responsible for making competitive decisions and formulating strategy to compete. Since most small firms, particularly family-owned small businesses, do not organize themselves like multi-national corporations with offices in various countries, they do not separate business strategy from corporate strategy. In a small business, corporate strategy and business strategy are blurred. Nevertheless, these businesses require a business strategy to increase their market share, profitability, performance, and growth.

Functional strategies or operational strategies occur at the lowest levels of the hierarchy within an organization. Functional or operational strategies are tactical in nature. Examples of operational or functional strategies are marketing strategy, pricing strategy, advertising strategy, human resources strategy, production strategy, financial strategy, purchasing strategy and so on. Operational or functional strategies support business strategy.

Attack, Cooperate, Ignore, Defend (ACID)

There are four main kinds of strategy actions called ACID strategy. The choice of a particular ACID will depend on a firm's resources and capabilities, internal strengths and weaknesses, or its external threats and opportunities. ACID strategy consists of:

- Attack
- Cooperate
- Ignore
- Defend

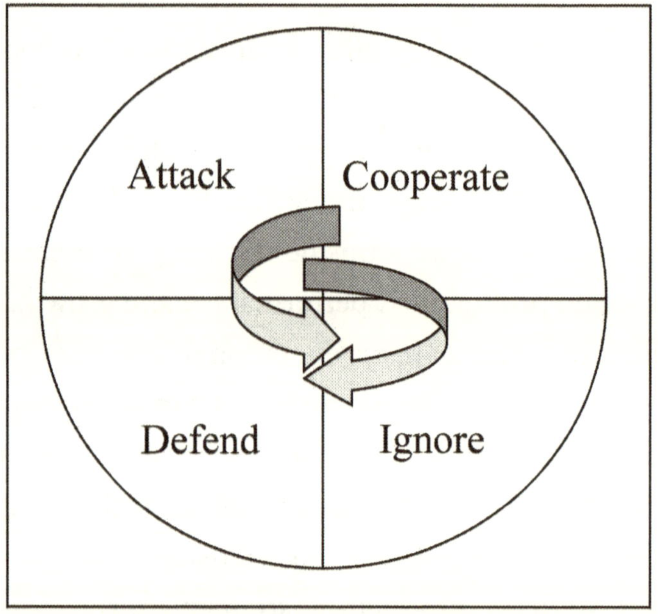

Figure 15: ACID Strategy

Firms which want to gain a bigger share of the market will use an attack strategy. An attack strategy can unseat an incumbent firm. Examples of attack strategies are differentiation through heavy advertising, promotion, product innovation, or pricing methods, to mention a few. Not all strategies have to be combative or competitive. Sometimes it makes sense for a firm to cooperate with a competitor rather than going into head-to-head competition. Firms use an ignore strategy when they do not see that the threats or opportunities in the business environment are significant enough to cause major harm to their firms. When under attack themselves, firms will invoke a defensive strategy. Even if not under attack, a firm will defend itself from potential attackers.

Depending on circumstances, a firm can use one, or a combination of the ACID as a strategy to compete. The choice of a particular ACID depends on many factors, including a firm's resources and capabilities, the risk tolerance of management, and strategy mindset. The type of ACID the firm selects must fit the vision, mission, and the personality of the firm.

Cost Strategy

Cost strategy is perhaps one of the oldest and most commonly used strategies. No business can expect to do well without applying some kind of a cost-control strategy. This is because, all things said and done, the profit a firm makes depends in part on the firm's ability to control its costs. Paying attention to the elements of a firm's cost is one way to control costs.

Elements of a firm's cost include:

- Direct material cost
- Indirect material cost

- Direct labour cost
- Overhead cost
- Selling cost
- General and administrative costs

A firm is able to increase its profits by lowering its cost. For example, a firm sells its product for $200. It costs $150 to produce the product. It makes a profit of $50 ($200 minus $150). In this simple case, if the firm decreases its cost by 50 percent, the firm can increase its profits to $125 ($200 minus $75).

Pricing Strategies

Three methods of pricing strategy are available to a firm. They are accounting-based pricing strategy (ABPS), market-based pricing strategy (MBPS), and economics-based pricing strategy (EBPS). The discussion that follows highlights each one of them.

Accounting-Based Pricing Strategy (ABPS)

Accounting-based pricing strategy assumes that firms are in business to make money and not for philanthropic reasons. Therefore, a firm must take into account the cost of producing an item as well as a margin towards profits. Several things make up the cost of production. Some of the cost considerations are:

- Labour cost
- Material cost
- Overhead costs
- Advertising costs
- Promotion costs

If a firm sells its products at cost, the firm makes zero profit. In order to make profits, a firm must sell what it produces at a price above the cost. For example, with ABPS, a firm can decide to price what it produces at 60 percent above the production cost. The 60 percent represents the desired profit margin (DPM). If the total production cost is $1,000 per item, then the firm can price its product at $1,600, as shown in Exhibit 13.

Exhibit 13: Accounting-based pricing strategy (ABPS)

Cost of production in dollars	
labor cost (wages, salaries, overtime)	300
material	300
overhead	200
advertising	100
promotion	100
total production cost	1,000
desired profit margin (DPM) - 60%	600
price of product	1,600

Market-Based Pricing Strategy (MBPS)

Market-based pricing strategy assumes that the price of a product is determined by what the "market will bear." Real estate is bought and sold with this method. In real estate, for example, a seller initially establishes the price of a house. A purchaser responds with a counter-price, being the price the purchaser is willing to pay. The seller may counter the price. This can go on until both the purchaser and the seller agree on a final price of the house. The final price is one that the purchaser is willing to pay and that the seller is willing to accept. The stock market falls into this category. Stock (share) prices open at a certain price, and sellers offer to sell their shares at a certain price; buyers must decide whether to accept or reject the price the seller offers. The final price is decided when both agree on a price. The owner has no control over how much the share will sell for, since this is determined by the market.

Economics-Based Pricing Strategy (EBPS)

Economics-based pricing strategy assumes that a firm has some control over the price and of the amount (quantity) it can sell of a product or a service. Although firms operating in perfect competition markets have little to no control, firms operating in monopolistic, oligopoly, and monopoly markets have some control over pricing of their products or services.

Monopolistic firms can differentiate their products or services from competitors, which allow them to price their products or services higher or lower than competitors. Oligopolies can form cartels, such as those found in the oil industry, to raise or lower prices, or restrict or increase production of oil. Similarly, monopolies are able to restrict output and raise prices.

Differentiation Strategy

Differentiation strategy serves to distinguish a firm and its products or services from competitors. A firm achieves differentiation when customers in its target market or industry perceive the firm and its products or services as unique.

A firm can be different from competitors in several ways, such as:

- Changing some attributes of its product or service. This can be accomplished through increasing reliability, durability, performance, or quality.
- Emphasizing the value of its services to customers, such as customer training, maintenance and repairs, and 24/7 service.
- Displaying employee skills such as, courtesy, professionalism, friendliness, and competence.
- Creating a company image using, symbols, sponsorship of special events, advertising, and public relations.

A firm that pursues a differentiation strategy is able to defend itself better against market forces such as threats of potential entrants, supplier threats, consumer threats, threats of substitutes, or threats of competitive rivalry. A differentiation strategy creates an entry barrier to future competitors, offers protection against competitive rivalry, minimizes supplier power, and reduces the threats of substitutes and consumer power. Furthermore, differentiation strategy allows a firm to create customer loyalty and increase product margins in order to earn above-average returns.

Michael Porter, a professor at Harvard University, cautions that differentiation can be incompatible sometimes with pursuit of market share. This is because differentiation strategy can sometimes create the impression that the product or service is offered to only a select group of customers who can afford to buy the product or service. The pursuit of higher market share objectives sometimes can also be in conflict with differentiation as a business strategy objective, especially when the cost of producing the products or services is high. Consumers may decide to purchase from a low cost producer at a lower price instead.

A firm that focuses on differentiation strategy is pursuing a niche marketing strategy. A niche marketing strategy focuses resources and marketing efforts on a narrowly defined market segment. This strategy allows a firm to target customers in a particular segment, to the exclusion of all other customers in the entire market. A firm that pursues differentiation strategy selects one or more attributes that buyers perceive as important to them. In this way, the firm can uniquely position itself to meet the needs of the select group of customers in the target market. This allows the firm to reward itself for its uniqueness by charging premium prices for its products or services. The ability to reward itself with premium prices permits the firm to make above-normal profits. How does your firm differentiate its products and services from competitors?

Market Positioning Strategy

A market positioning strategy is a psychological marketing technique that firms use to create value and a superior image in the minds of target consumers. A positioning strategy conditions the target market about a firm's unique value proposition and the reasons why the target customers should purchase the firm's products or services. This allows a firm to distinguish its products and services from all other competitors in the minds of buyers.

Resource-based Strategy

Resource-based strategy focuses on identifying, developing, and deploying a firm's resources in a way that allows the firm to earn above-average returns, increase market share, or improve overall performance results. The premise of resource-based strategy is that the resources a firm controls and fully exploits determine the level of the firm's performance. The manner in which a firm uses its resources and capabilities to compete determines the firm's competitive advantage or sustainable competitive advantage.

Firms differ in the types of resources they possess. Different firms develop and deploy resources differently to achieve above-average returns and gain sustainable competitive advantage. The benefit derived from the resources must be greater than the cost of acquiring and using the resources. A firm's performance is determined, in part, by how the firm acquires, develops, and deploys resources. A firm that has a competitive advantage or sustainable competitive advantage generally earns above-average returns within its industry.

Business Combination Strategy

Many forms of business combination exist. These include integration, mergers, acquisition, and consolidation. Integration occurs when productive resources of firms are brought together to achieve a desired business objective. The two main types of integration are vertical integration and horizontal integration. These forms of business combination will be discussed in this chapter.

Vertical Integration Strategy

A vertical integration occurs when two or more firms combine resources and capabilities to produce a single product or service that involves two or more successive production or distribution stages. A vertically integrated strategy permits a firm to gain more control over resources and various stages of production and distribution of the final products. This allows a firm to bypass firms that supply various inputs and capabilities. The firm is no longer dependent on other firms to supply its required inputs and capability. It becomes capable of supplying and producing the required inputs internally.

Consider for example, a chocolate manufacturer who initially depends on cocoa-producing farmers to supply cocoa beans, and a cocoa processing factory to process the beans into cocoa powder and cocoa butter. These activities or stages of production feed into the manufacturing process of the chocolates. The firm will pursue vertical integration strategy when it decides to own or control the various stages in the manufacturing processes of the chocolate. The vertically integrated chocolate manufacturer, in this case, can now obtain its cocoa beans from the cocoa farm, which it now owns, and processes its own cocoa powder and cocoa butter from the cocoa processing factory, which it controls. The chocolate manufacturer can also own and control the distribution channels for the finished goods (chocolates).

A non-vertically integrated chocolate manufacturing firm, in contrast with a vertically integrated firm, would not own a cocoa farm, a cocoa bean processing plant, or a distribution channel. The firm would buy all its production inputs and distribution services from outside sources. It would buy cocoa beans from cocoa farmers, cocoa powder and cocoa butter from cocoa processing manufacturers, and engage the services of distributors. Firms that buy inputs or services from other firms are non-vertically integrated.

Other forms of vertical integration are forward-vertical integration and backward-vertical integration. One way to explain forward-vertical integration and backward-vertical integration is to imagine a river flowing from upstream to downstream. Assume that there is a finished good (chocolate) manufacturing firm located in between the upstream and downstream sections of the river. Located in the upstream section of the river is a raw materials supply firm (cocoa farmer). In the downstream of the river are chocolate distribution firms and chocolate retail stores. The firms in the downstream are very close to the final consumer.

When a manufacturing firm joins with a firm located downstream, such that the firm gets closer to the consumer, the firm is engaging in forward-vertical integration. For example, if a chocolate manufacturer joins with a transport firm, a warehouse firm, or retail store to make products and services available to consumers, this chocolate manufacturer is using forward-vertical integration strategy.

On the other hand, a manufacturing firm that joins with another firm in the upstream, such as raw material suppliers, is pursuing backward-vertical integration. A firm that controls the supply of raw materials in the upstream is pursuing backward-vertical integration. For example, a chocolate manufacturer that owns cocoa farms that supply cocoa beans is using a backward-vertical integration strategy.

The number of production and distribution stages that a firm controls determines the level of integration of the firm. The more stages of production and distribution a firm controls, the more the firm is vertically integrated. On the other hand, the fewer the number of stages in the production and distribution the firm controls, the less the firm is vertically integrated.

A firm can estimate its level of vertical integration based on information contained in its financial statements. According to J.B Barney, the level of vertical integration can be determined by dividing a firm's value-added by its sales, and then expressing the result in a percentage. The higher the percentage, the more vertically integrated a firm is. On the other hand, the lower the percentage, the less vertically integrated a firm is.

Horizontal Integration Strategy

Horizontal integration occurs when two firms, each producing similar or substitute products or services, integrate into a single firm. An example of a horizontal integration is when two aircraft manufacturers, such as Boeing and McDonnell Douglas, integrate into a single firm called Boeing-McDonnell. Similarly, if two soft drink firms integrate into a single firm, they are pursuing a horizontal integration since each of their products is a substitute for each other.

In comparison to a vertical integration where inputs (raw materials) and various production stages are completed under the roof of a single firm, horizontal integration brings finished products or services under the roof of a single firm.

Merger, Acquisition, and Consolidation

A merger is a combination of two or more firms where one firm acquires another firm or firms. The purchase of the other firm is an acquisition. The combination of the firms is a merger or consolidation. Merger, acquisition, and consolidation are all forms of integration.

A merger involves the combination of two or more firms to form an entirely new firm. The acquiring firm buys or absorbs the target firm. The acquiring firm retains its identity and the acquired firm ceases to exist. In a merger situation, the acquiring firm is usually larger than the target firm. Thus, when two firms are not of equal size, they merge. There are several types of mergers; horizontal merger, vertical merger, conglomerate merger, product extension merger, and market extension merger.

A horizontal merger occurs when a firm acquires its direct competitor. For example, if two competing banks such as Royal Bank and Scotia Bank or two oil firms such as Exxon and Mobil were to merge, that would be a horizontal merger.

A vertical merger occurs when a firm acquires its supplier of raw materials or its distributors. For example, a chocolate manufacturer buys a cocoa-producing firm. In contrast, a conglomerate merger is a combination of firms in completely unrelated markets or industries. For example, a merger between a cable television firm and a car-manufacturing firm will result in a conglomerate merger. A product extension merger involves a situation where a firm acquires another firm that produces complementary products. A merger between a tire-manufacturing firm and an automobile manufacturer would be a good example of a product extension merger. The aim is to gain access into a complementary product market. The merger between AT&T and McCaw Cellular telephone is a good example of this. The merger allowed AT&T to gain entry into the cellular phone product market.

Lastly, a market extension merger is a combination between firms with the purpose of gaining entry into new geographic markets. For example, the acquisition of Air Touch and Mannesmann by Vodafone allowed Vodafone to expand its geographic markets beyond its domestic markets in United Kingdom.

Cooperation Strategy

Cooperation strategy is an alternative to direct competition with a rival firm. Firms need not be rivals at all times. Instead, a firm can choose to cooperate with another firm to pursue a common business objective. Many forms of co-operation strategy exist. The two main types of cooperation strategy are collusion and alliance.

Collusion Strategy

Collusion occurs when a few dominant firms in an industry agree (directly or indirectly) through their actions to reduce competition in that industry. This can happen through restricting outputs or production (supply) and raising prices of the firms' products or services. For collusion to occur there must be only a few dominant firms in the industry (oligopoly). These firms must be in the position to restrict outputs, charge higher prices, make above-normal profits for their products or services, and restrict competition. There are two kinds of collusion strategy, which are explicit collusion and tacit collusion.

Both explicit collusion and tacit collusion strategies can have adverse effects on competition. Explicit collusion strategy occurs when two or more firms formally cooperate through negotiation to reduce production and to set the prices to charge consumers, with the objective to reduce competition within their industry. Firms can also cooperate without having to negotiate formally on output restriction or setting prices for their products or services by observing the behaviour of their main competitors with respect to their outputs and their pricing decisions. Tacit collusion occurs when firms coordinate production levels and pricing decisions to limit competition within an industry without having to formally agree on how much to produce or charge for their products or services. Any form of collusion that restricts output in order to increase prices that benefits only a few firms at the expense of consumers is generally frown upon by government officials.

Alliance

An alliance strategy exists when two or more firms that are independent cooperate to combine their resources, capabilities, or core competencies to pursue mutually beneficial business goals that would be hard for an individual firm to achieve alone.

A firm can pursue this strategy through a non-equity alliance, an equity alliance, a joint venture, or a complementary alliance. A non-equity alliance is a contractual arrangement between firms that permits a company to manufacture, supply, or distribute products or services without equity participation. No equity arrangements are involved.

An equity alliance occurs when two or more firms or organizations cooperate in developing, manufacturing, or selling their products or services. In equity alliance, the firms involved supplement contracts with equity holdings. The partners in equity alliance own different percentages of equity holdings.

In a joint venture, two or more firms or organizations cooperate to create an independent firm for mutual benefit. Each firm or organization owns an equal share in the company they have created, and share equally in any profits that come from the alliance as compensation for their investments.

A complementary alliance occurs when firms or organizations cooperate to combine their assets in a complementary manner in order to create value and take advantage of market opportunities for mutually beneficial business goals.

There are many reasons for using an alliance as a preferred strategy, including the following:

- Gain market access
- Learn and acquire expertise in marketing or gain capabilities in distribution channels
- Get around trade barriers
- Gain entry into lucrative markets
- Focus resources in areas of competitive advantage
- Respond quickly to rapidly changing business environment
- Achieve better and faster financial performance results
- Improve the time it takes to bring products or services to market

Steps to developing an alliance are:

Step 1: Define goals and objectives for the alliance.
Step 2: Search for potential partners.
Step 3: Select a partner.
Step 4: Negotiate with the alliance partner.
Step 5: Monitor the alliance.
Step 6: Manage the alliance.
Step 7: Conduct ongoing or regular communication with the partner.

An alliance must have its goals and objectives clearly defined. For example, the goals and objectives could be a joint marketing of products or services as in a pharmaceutical industry, to co-develop a drug for approval and sale within five years.

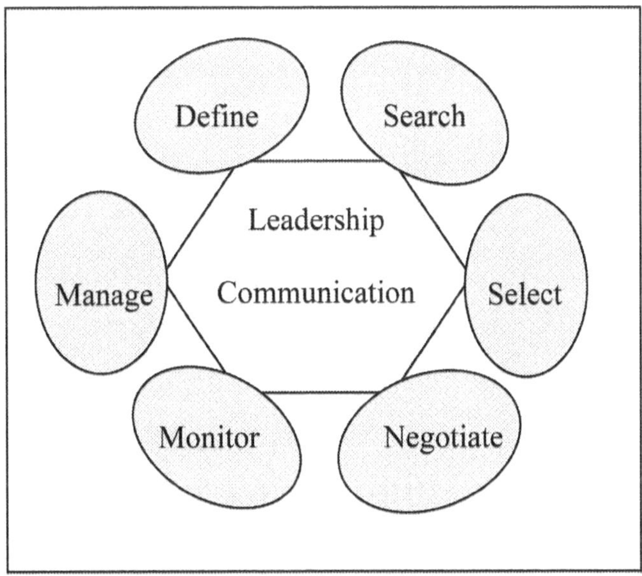

Figure 16: Alliance Development Model (ADM)

A search for the right partner is critical to an alliance. All parties to an alliance must be committed to the desired goals and objectives. This must include resource commitment.

Monitoring and managing the alliance allows it to flourish. In this way, things will stay on track. More importantly, there should be an ongoing communication between partners so that any misunderstandings can be readily resolved. Leadership is essential in focusing the alliance partners to the desired goals and objectives.

Mission and Vision Strategy

Mission and vision strategy create shared expectations, a sense of common identity, shared values, and establish behaviour standards for a firm. They serve as overall guidelines for decisions regarding strategy, competition, customers, human resources, resource allocation, and competencies, to name a few.

No standard definition exists for mission or vision in the business world. A mission can be whatever a firm or organization wants it to be. It can contain elements of the firm's strategy, behaviour standards, values, products, market, and technology that are seen as reflecting the objectives of the organization.

A clearly defined mission statement has many benefits. It provides firms with a clear direction, serves as a basis for a common purpose and shared values. It builds a common understanding among those who have a stake in the firm. These include employees, managers, and shareholders. A vision, on the other hand, is a big mental picture of where the firm wants to be in the future. The vision must reflect the aspirations and dreams of the leader of the firm, such as the president, CEO, or the business owner.

A firm's actions should align with its mission and vision. Mission and vision co-exist in firms and organizations. Every firm has a mission or vision, whether written or unwritten. Mission and vision are the glue that enables a firm to achieve its business objectives. In order to succeed, a firm's mission, vision, values, and strategy must fit together like a jigsaw puzzle.

Benefits of Business Strategy

Businesses compete for customers. Customers must be at the center of a business strategy. No firm can survive without customers. The objective of firms is to maximize some desired business objective, such as return on invested capital (ROIC), return on investment (ROI), sales revenues, market share, profitability, or overall performance. While some firms are successful at achieving their desired business objectives, others are not.

Firms that achieve above-normal performance or their desired business objectives do so through a deliberate strategy. Firms that use strategy, written or unwritten, to compete are able to achieve higher levels of performance than those that do not. Firms such as IBM, Microsoft, Wal-Mart, Coca-Cola, and Pepsi have one thing in common; they all use a business strategy to compete.

A firm that has no business strategy will most likely be shooting in the dark. Without a business strategy, defeat in the competitive arena and bankruptcy is almost certain. Bankruptcy creates hardships for firms, entrepreneurs, and investors, as well as individuals and their families who depend on a firm for livelihood. The economic, social, and psychological impacts of bankruptcies are enormous. A careful and effective business strategy can help prevent the possibility of bankruptcy.

A firm thrives when it is profitable and enjoys above-normal performance. Investors are attracted to firms that are profitable. When a company is profitable, it can command higher share prices than those who earn below-normal profits. A business strategy helps firms achieve greater market share and higher return on invested capital, earn above-normal profits, and achieve higher overall performance. A business strategy allows firms to identify their competitive advantage or strategic competitive advantage, to exploit their strengths, capitalize on opportunities, and minimize threats and weaknesses that constrain their ability to compete to win. A business strategy is to a firm as an engine is to a vehicle. Without an engine, a vehicle will not move. Similarly, a firm without a business strategy can stagnate and eventually collapse into bankruptcy.

PART III

Strategy Decisions and Performance

Chapter 6

Strategy Decisions

Managers and executives face strategy decisions regularly. Sometimes strategy decisions are made in circumstances where the managers and executives have full knowledge or information about the circumstances in which the decisions are to be made. Other times, strategic decisions occur within the context of experience. Yet in other situations, there is no past experience or past data to guide strategy decisions. Regardless of the circumstances, managerial and executive decisions affect a firm negatively or positively. A good strategy decision can contribute to a firm's success; a bad one can lead a firm into bankruptcy. Whatever decision a firm makes, it will have financial implications and sometimes far-reaching consequences.

The results of strategy decisions show up directly or indirectly in a firm's financial statements. Financial statements, such as the income statement and the balance sheet, report the results of a firm's performance. The ability of a firm to achieve its desired objectives depends largely on the quality of decisions its management makes. These decisions must translate into economic and financial performance results.

This chapter discusses different circumstances under which strategy decisions are made. This can improve the chances of making better decisions and contribute to the development of a strategy mindset for achieving better and faster results.

Types of Strategy Decisions

Strategy decisions involve actions a firm takes with the view of reaping benefits in the future. These benefits could involve future cash flows, higher profits, growth, market share, or performance. Circumstances that give rise to strategy decisions include but are not limited to the following:

- Product development
- Marketing
- Mergers
- Acquisitions
- Integration
- Competitive positioning
- Capital budgeting
- Investments
- Operations
- Dividend
- Foreign market entry
- Capital assets

In reality, firms make strategy decisions in situations with some degree of certainty, risk, or uncertainty. Thus, strategy decisions can be grouped as follows:

- Strategy decisions under certainty
- Strategy decisions under risk
- Strategy decisions under uncertainty

Strategy Decision Under Certainty (SDUC)

In strategy decisions under certainty, a person making the decision has full and complete information in advance about what will happen (the event), the chances of it happening (the probability), and the consequences of it happening (the outcomes). As an example to illustrate strategy decision under certainty, consider union-management wage negotiations illustrated in Exhibit 14.

Exhibit 14: Strategy decision under certainty	
Strategy 1	5 percent wage increase
Strategy 2	6 percent wage increase
Strategy 3	7 percent wage increase

Mini case:

Union workers are threatening to go on strike unless the union reaches a wage settlement with management at the negotiating table. The union will accept a wage offer from management, if the offer is reasonable. The union members will vote on any wage offer from management. The union members and management will reach a settlement when the negotiated wage is acceptable to both parties.

Management faces three strategy options: Strategy 1, Strategy 2, and Strategy 3, as shown in Exhibit 14. Management has full and complete information about the event and is 100 percent certain of what the union will accept or reject during the negotiation.

Management is certain that the union will accept a wage increase of between 5 percent minimum and 7 percent maximum. Management is fully certain that the union will reject any wage settlement ranging from between 0 percent to 4.9 percent. Armed with this information in advance of heading to the negotiation table, management can choose any of the three strategy options. For example, management can choose the Strategy 1 option, an offer of a 5 percent wage increase. Management can also pursue the Strategy 2 option, where it is certain that the union members will accept a 6 percent wage increase. Similar reasoning applies to the Strategy 3 option, where management knows that the union members will accept a 7 percent wage increase. Naturally, a profit-maximizing firm will no doubt pursue Strategy 1, because that is the least cost option to the firm that the union will accept.

In this case, management was hundred percent certain about what the union members would accept or reject in their wage settlement. The likelihood (probability) of the union members accepting the Strategy 1 option was highly likely. Management can assign a probability of one to Strategy 1, knowing that there was a hundred percent chance that the union members will accept it.

(Note that probability ranges between zero, meaning the likelihood (chances) of something (event) happening is zero (meaning it will not happen), to one, meaning there is hundred percent chance (likelihood) that something (event) will happen. A probability cannot be less than zero or more than one)).

Strategy Decision Under Risk (SDUR)

A strategy decision under risk is about the chance or likelihood that something bad would happen. The chance (probability) of this bad thing (event) occurring is estimated using prior experience of seeing or hearing about this bad thing having happened before. Therefore, the probability associated with the risk depends on past observations of the same or a similar event having occurred. In this case, the probability is objective, since it is estimated from experience or observation.

As an illustration of decision-making under risk, consider a firm that builds family homes. Based on experience or data on previous years' home sales, the firm has been able to establish probabilities for the demand for homes as high, moderate, or low. The probabilities associated with high, moderate, or low demand for homes are 0.30, 0.20, and 0.50 respectively. The types of homes the firm wants to build are four-bedroom homes, three-bedroom homes, or two-bedroom condominium homes. The firm has limited resources and has decided to build only one type of home. This means that if the firm decides to build four-bedroom homes, it will not have funds available to build three-bedroom homes or two-bedroom homes. Similarly, if the firm decides to build three-bedroom homes, no funds will be available for four-bedroom homes or the condominiums, and so on.

Exhibit 15 shows the estimated revenues from the sale of different types of homes and the probabilities associated with high, moderate, and low demand for housing. Strategy 1, Strategy 2, and Strategy 3 correspond to building four-bedroom homes, three-bedroom homes, or two-bedroom condominiums respectively.

Exhibit 15: Strategy decision under risk

	Demand for Housing		
	High demand (0.30) (in million dollars)	**Moderate demand (0.20) (in million dollars)**	**Low demand (0.50) (in million dollars)**
Strategy 1: Build four-bedroom homes	$25	$20	$5
Strategy 2: Build three-bedroom homes	$25	$15	$15
Strategy 3: Build two-bedroom homes	$20	$20	$10

The business problem that the firm faces is to decide on which strategy will generate optimum revenues for the firm under different levels of demand for housing. If the firm decides to build four-bedroom homes and demand for homes is high, the firm would generate $25 million in sales. The probability that demand for four-bedroom homes will be high is 0.30. On the other hand, if the demand for homes were moderate, the sales revenues for four-bedroom home would produce $20 million. The likelihood that the demand for four-bedroom homes would be moderate is 0.20. If the demand for four-bedroom homes happens to be low, the firm would receive $5 million in sales revenues. The probability associated with low demand for four-bedroom homes is 0.50. The same reasoning is used for Strategy 2 (building three-bedroom homes) and Strategy 3 (building two-bedroom condominium homes).

To decide on which type of homes to build under various levels of demand, the firm must calculate the expected monetary value (EMV) for each type of home. The homes with the highest expected monetary revenue value would be the recommended strategy.

To estimate the expected monetary value (EMV) for each home to build, follow the following steps:

Step 1: Set up a table similar to the one in Exhibit 15.

Step 2: Multiply the probability associated with high demand for housing by the estimated sales revenues when demand for housing is high. Refer to Exhibit 16, column two–row one.

Step 3: Multiply the probability associated with moderate demand for housing by the estimated sales revenues when demand for housing is moderate. Refer to Exhibit16, column three - row one.

Step 4: Multiply the probability associated with low demand for housing by the estimated sales revenues when demand for housing is low. Refer to Exhibit 16, column four - row one.

Step 5: Add the results of the calculations to obtain the expected monetary value (EMV). Refer to Exhibit 16, column five - row one.

Step 6: Do similar calculations for Strategy 2 (three-bedroom homes types) and Strategy 3 (two-bedroom condominiums).

Step 7: Select the strategy with the largest expected monetary value (EMV) as in Exhibit 16, column five.

According to these calculations, the strategy to recommend is Strategy 2, since it produces the largest amount of expected monetary value ($18 million) compared to the EMV for Strategy 1 ($14 million) or Strategy 3 ($15 million).

Exhibit 16: Expected monetary values (EMV) for housing demand

	High demand (0.30) (in million dollars)	**Moderate demand (0.20) (in million dollars)**	**Low demand (0.50) (in million dollars)**	**Expected monetary values (EMV) (in million dollars)**
Strategy 1	$7.5 (0.30 x $25)	$4 (0.20 x $20)	$2.5 (0.50 x $5)	$14
Strategy 2	$7.5 (0.30 x 25)	$3 (0.20 x $15)	$7.5 (0.50 x $15)	**$18**
Strategy 3	$6 (0.30 x $20)	$4 (0.20 x $20)	$5 (0.50 x $10)	$15

Strategy Decision Under Uncertainty (SDUU)

Strategy decisions under uncertainty occur in situations where there is no previous experience on which to base the decisions. The likelihood (probability) that an event would occur depends on a hunch basis, in which case the probability assigned is subjective.

As an illustration of SDUU, consider Exhibit 17.

Exhibit 17: Strategy decision under uncertainty

	High demand	Moderate demand	Low demand
Strategy 1: Import Lexus salon cars	$400,000	$200,000	$50,000
Strategy 2: Import Mercedes Benz salon cars	$600,000	$300,000	$40,000
Strategy 3: Import BMW salon cars	$200,000	$200,000	$60,000

A car dealer is considering importing salon cars: Lexus, Mercedes Benz, or BMW. The owner of the car dealership has estimated sales revenues under three scenarios of high demand, moderate demand, and low demand for these cars. For example, if demand for cars were high, the dealer would be able to sell $400,000 worth of Lexus salon cars, $600,000 worth of Mercedes Benz salon cars, or $200,000 worth of BMW salon cars. If demand were moderate, the dealer would make $200,000 on Lexus, $300,000 on Mercedes Benz, or $200,000 on BMW. Interpret the rest of the amounts in Exhibit 17 in the same way.

The car dealer must decide on which type of salon car to import. Strategy 1, Strategy 2, and Strategy 3 correspond to importation of Lexus salon cars, Mercedes Benz salon cars, and BMW salon cars respectively. Unlike strategy decisions under risk, which uses objective probabilities in the calculations, strategy decisions under uncertainty do not contain objective probabilities associated with high demand, moderate demand, or low demand. Rather it uses subjective probabilities. Subjective probability is an estimate of one's hunch.

The choice of strategy will depend on whether the car dealer is optimistic or pessimistic about the condition of demand. Assume for a moment that the car dealer is an optimist. This being the case, the car dealer will consider the most optimistic payoff or outcomes under the most favourable demand conditions. For example, the biggest revenues or payoffs happen under the condition of high demand. Under the condition of high demand, Strategy 1 would generate $400,000; Strategy 2 would produce $600,000, while Strategy 3 would yield $200,000. The car dealer, being an optimist, will select Strategy 2, since the payoff is the largest.

Under this strategy decision, a profit maximizing decision-maker, who is an optimist, will import Mercedes Benz salon cars since it will generate sales revenues of $600,000. Refer to Strategy 2 as shown in Exhibit 18.

Exhibit 18: Strategy decision for an optimist	
	Maximum revenues when demand is high
Strategy 1: Import Lexus salon cars	$400,000
Strategy 2: Import Mercedes Benz salon cars	**$600,000**
Strategy 3: Import BMW salon cars	$200,000

A pessimistic decision-maker, on the other hand, would base decisions on the worst-case scenario, as shown in Exhibit 19. The worst-case scenario is when the demand is low, in which case Strategy 1 would generate $50,000, Strategy 2 would produce $40,000, and Strategy 3 would yield $60,000. The cautious pessimist would select Strategy 3 since by importing BMW under this worst-case, the car dealership generates revenues of at least $60,000.

Exhibit 19: Strategy decision for a pessimist	
	Maximum revenues when demand is low
Strategy 1: Import Lexus salon cars	$50,000
Strategy 2: Import Mercedes Benz salon cars	$40,000
Strategy 3: Import BMW salon cars	**$60,000**

Management Decisions

Management decisions show up in two basic financial statements, called the income statement and the balance sheet. There are four kinds of management decisions:

- Investment decisions
- Operating decisions
- Financing decisions
- Dividend decisions

Investment decisions affect the assets of a firm. Assets consist of current assets, non-current or fixed assets, and intangible assets. Current assets are cash or cash equivalent assets. Cash equivalent assets are those assets that a firm can convert into cash on a short notice. Examples of current assets are cash, marketable securities, accounts receivable, inventories, and prepaid expenses. Non-current or fixed assets, on the other hand, can take longer to convert into cash. Examples of non-current assets include land, buildings, equipment, and machinery. Intangible assets usually consist of intellectual property rights (IPR) such as patents, trade-marks, industrial design, and copyrights.

Typically, investment decisions are concerned with the risks associated with acquiring, keeping, and liquidating assets, allocating resources, and managing resources. Operating decisions affect the income statement of a firm's financial reports. The income statement is a summary of a firm's revenues, expenses, and profits or losses. A firm makes profits when its revenues exceed its expenses. A firm incurs losses when the firm's expenses are greater than its revenues. A firm can increase its profits by increasing its prices or by lowering its expenses (costs).

Financing decisions involve decisions about a firm's equities. A firm's equities consist of liabilities and owners' equity. Owners' equity is the amount owners have invested in the firm. Liabilities are claims against the firm's assets by creditors. They represent financial obligations or amounts owed to lenders, such as banks, bondholders, government agencies, suppliers, and financial obligations to workers such as unpaid wages.

A firm's liabilities consist of current liabilities and long-term liabilities. Current liabilities are amounts owed by the firm that the firm must pay within a year. Examples of current liabilities are accounts payable (amount owed to suppliers), notes payable, taxes payable, accrued expenses (such as interest payable and wages payable), and deferred revenues (such as magazine subscriptions collected in advance). Long-term liabilities are amounts owed that will not be paid within the current year. The payment period can span over several years. Examples of long-term liabilities are mortgages, long-term loans, and long-term leases.

Typically, financing decisions must consider short-term financing, intermediate financing, long-term financing, and optimum financing mix or capital structure.

Dividend decisions involve the distribution of a firm's profits to its shareholders (stockholders). These decisions require a balance between distributing the profits the firm makes to shareholders, and keeping the profits within the firm. A firm that has many undistributed profits is able to take advantage of market opportunities without necessarily resorting to external borrowing. It can choose to finance a strategy project from its own earnings. However, some shareholders could be unhappy if they do not receive dividend over a long period.

Some investors prefer cash dividends while others prefer retaining earnings in the firm in the hope of selling their shares in the future at higher prices. The decision-maker must balance the needs of the firm against those investors who want stock appreciation and those who want cash dividends. Another critical issue that a decision-maker faces is when to finance investment projects without using external sources of funds and when to use the firm's own fund to finance strategy projects.

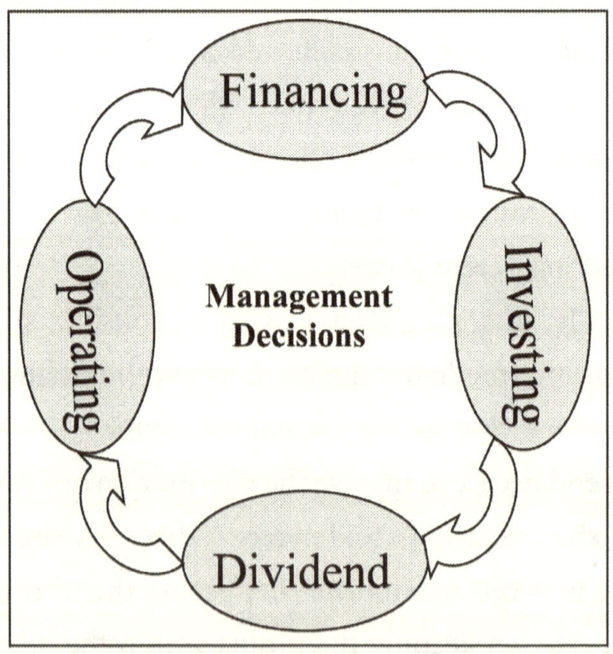

Figure 17: Management Decisions

Investing decisions, operating decisions, financing decisions, and dividend decisions affect each other. Consider, for example, a firm's decision to build a warehouse. This decision will involve financing decisions. It will require the firm to borrow money from a financial institution to finance the construction of the warehouse. The finished warehouse is an investment to create an asset (building), which increases the total assets value of the firm. By borrowing from the financial institution to finance the construction of the warehouse, it allowed the firm to, perhaps, meet its dividend payout obligations. The warehouse will require maintenance and interest payments on the borrowed money. This again will involve operating decisions. The decision to build a warehouse created a chain reaction affecting financing, dividends, investing, and operating decisions, as illustrated in Figure 17.

Chapter 7

Strategy Performance Measures

A firm is successful when it is performing well. When a firm is not performing well, it is stagnating or unsuccessful. Central to business strategy is how well a firm performs or how successful it is in achieving its performance objectives. A firm exists to make money and create value for its customers and shareholders. It uses its productive assets such as money (capital), labour, management skills, buildings, machinery, technology, people, raw materials, resources, and capabilities to achieve its desired objectives.

There are several ways to measure the success of a firm. The level of profitability, growth, productivity, and overall performance are among those that can indicate a firm's success. When a firm is making more money, through the sale of its products and services, it is performing well. A firm that is increasing its market share is growing. On the other hand, if a firm is losing market share to competitors and making less money, it is experiencing a decline in growth.

However, the caution is that even when a firm is increasing its market share it does not necessarily follow that the firm is profitable. A firm that is able to generate more revenues with its assets is more productive than the one that produces fewer revenues with its productive assets. Examples of productive assets are equipment, buildings, machinery or similar resources.

Financial ratios, derived from a firm's financial statements, can signal how well a firm is performing with respect to growth, profitability, productivity, and overall performance. A firm's performance can produce three possible outcomes: normal performance, below-normal performance, and above-normal performance.

Normal performance occurs when a business is neither making money nor losing money. When this occurs, the firm is breaking even. In this situation, the firm is making normal profits. Firms that earn normal profits have little or no competitive advantage over their competitors. When this happens, the firm must put in place a business strategy that will end the normal profit syndrome.

Below-normal performance happens when a firm is neither making normal profits nor above-normal profits. A firm that finds itself in this situation is losing money and performing poorly. The firm has compromised its ability to compete. If the situation persists, the firm would soon face bankruptcy and go out of business. An effective strategy can reverse this poor performance.

Above-normal performance occurs when a firm's revenues exceed its expenses or costs. A firm that has above-normal performance is indeed making money and performing well. When a firm's revenues exceed its expenses, the firm makes profits. As a simple illustration, a firm that spends $30 to make a product that sells for $100 will make a profit of $70. In this simple illustration, the firm is making above-normal profit. Its revenues exceed expenses. Decisions must focus on the things the firm does well, what it must improve, what it must continue doing, and what it must stop doing in order to continue to enjoy above-normal performance.

Financial Performance Measures (FPM)

Financial statements report on a firm's financial performance to internal and external audiences. Internal audiences include a firm's divisional or line managers, senior management, and employee representatives such as union members. External audiences consist of investors, investment advisors, and creditors such as banks and suppliers. The two basic financial statements are the balance sheet, and the income statement.

The balance sheet reports on what a firm owns and what it owes at a particular point in time. The balance sheet shows the monetary amounts of resources that the firm has and the financial obligations against the firm. Resources that a firm owns are assets. These consist of tangible and intangible assets. Examples of tangible assets are cash, accounts receivable, investments (stocks and other securities), prepaid expenses, inventories, land, buildings, machinery, and equipment. Examples of intangible assets are goodwill and intellectual property rights, such as copyrights, patents, trademarks, and similar assets that are not tangible in nature.

What a firm owes are liabilities. They are claims against the assets of the firm. They represent the firm's financial obligations to creditors. Financial obligations include amounts of money the firm borrows from a financial institution, suppliers, or creditors.

Owners' equity on a balance sheet represents the residual interest of the owners of the firm. Residual interest refers to the fact that in situations of bankruptcy, a firm must pay back all the amounts of money it owes to creditors, and whatever remains after that, would go to the owners of the business. The owners' equity arises from financial contributions to the firm by owners and from the accumulation of the firm's profits. Owners' equity is equivalent to shareholders' equity or stockholders' equity of incorporated firms. For unincorporated businesses, the balance sheet reports owners' equity as owners' capital or capital invested by the owner.

The income statement shows the revenues the firm has earned and the expenses it has incurred over a given duration. Revenues are generally inflow of cash from the sale of the firm's products or services. Expenses are mostly an outflow of cash from the firm. Typically, items found on income statements are sales revenues, cost of goods sold, gross margin, general and selling expenses, income tax expense, depreciation expense, and net profit. The difference between a firm's total revenues and total expenses results in either profit or loss for the firm.

Total Revenues - Total Expenses = Profits

For example, a firm sells its products and generates total revenues of $365,000. The firm incurs total expenses of $165,000. The firm makes a profit of $200,000 ($365,000 - $165,000 = $200,000).

Financial Ratios

Most financial ratios are expressed in different ways such as, percentages, ratios, days, and "times" and so on. For example, the ratio of 20 apples and 4 oranges is 5:1 (20 divided by 4). Financial ratios are calculated in the same manner.

A firm calculates most of its financial ratios from the balance sheet and the income statement. It uses them to measure its financial performance and the quality of management decisions. Financial ratios can signal whether a firm is improving or deteriorating in performance when compared to its prior years' performance or to the average performance of the firm's industry. A firm's performance depends on its strategy and the kinds of decisions management makes.

Different groups of people use financial ratios for different purposes. For example, lenders such as banks focus on a firm's ability to generate enough cash to meet its financial obligations and remain solvent. The investment community is interested, among other things, on the firm's overall performance and its ability to make more profits.

The four main kinds of financial ratios, as shown in Exhibit 20, are:

- Financial condition ratios
- Investment utilization ratios
- Profitability ratios
- Overall performance ratios

Exhibit 20: Financial ratios			
Financial condition ratios	**Investment utilization ratios**	**Profitability ratios**	**Overall performance ratios**
• Current ratio • Quick ratio • Debt to equity ratio • Interest coverage ratio • Average interest rate ratio • Long-term debt to equity ratio • Debt to total assets ratio	• Total asset turnover ratio • Inventory turnover ratio • Invested capital turnover ratio • Working capital turnover ratio • Equity turnover ratio • Receivable collection period	• Profit margin ratio • Gross profit margin ratio • Earnings per share ratio	• Return on equity (ROE) ratio • Return on assets (ROA) ratio • Return on invested capital ratio (ROIC) • Price to earnings ratio • Return on capital employed ratio (ROCE) • Return on net asset ratio (RONA)

Financial ratios by themselves are meaningless. To be meaningful, a firm must compare its financial ratios with those of the industry in which it operates. A comparison with industry ratios can reveal whether a firm is doing better or worse. This will allow the firm to identify any weaknesses and highlight strengths. A firm can also compare its current year's performance with previous years' performances to determine where it needs improvement. Exhibit 21 shows some examples of financial condition ratios, investment utilization ratios, profitability ratios, and overall performance ratios of a hypothetical firm.

Exhibit 21: Financial ratios of XYZ Inc.

	Current Year	Year 3	Year 2	Year 1	Industry ratios	Worse (W)/ Better (B)
Financial condition ratios						
Current ratio	2.00	1.80	1.70	1.60	**1.50**	Better
Quick ratio	1.75	1.65	1.60	1.50	**1.40**	Better
Interest coverage ratio	35.00	32.50	29.50	25.80	**20.60**	Better
Debt to equity ratio	0.50	0.48	0.45	0.40	**0.90**	Better
Long-term debt to equity ratio	0.17	0.18	0.19	0.20	**0.25**	Better
Debt to total assets ratio	0.33	0.45	0.50	0.60	**0.80**	Better
Investment utilization ratios						
Total asset turnover ratio	3.33	3.60	3.80	3.90	**4.15**	**Worse**
Inventory turnover ratio	24.00	25.80	26.25	30.55	**35.50**	**Worse**
Profitability ratios						
Profit margin ratio	18.13%	18.25%	17.50%	16.25%	**14.50%**	Better
Gross profit margin ratio	60%	55%	50%	45%	**30.00%**	Better
Earnings per share ratio (EPS)	$3.63	$3.25	$3.15	$2.25	**$1.50**	Better
Overall performance ratios						
Return on invested capital (ROIC)	50.67%	45.80%	40.50%	35.90%	**30.50%**	Better
Return on net assets (RONA)	62.22%	60.52%	55.25%	50.25%	**45.56%**	Better

Most of this hypothetical firm's financial ratios look better than the industry average. The only areas where the firm is showing some weaknesses are in the investment utilization ratios, namely the total asset turnover ratio and inventory turnover ratio. The total asset turnover ratio (sales divided by total assets) is actually worsening, and when compared to industry average, the firm is doing poorly. The firm's asset turnover ratios are lower than the industry ratio. A low asset turnover ratio is an indication of an inefficient use of a firm's assets. The reason could be due to declining sales or high acquisition of assets by a firm. The firm can improve efficiencies by improving the amount of sales or getting rid of assets that do not add value to the firm's performance. The ratios have been worsening since Year 1.

Inventory turnover ratio (cost of goods sold divided by inventories) is also below the industry average and not improving. The inventory turnover represents the number of times a firm's inventory actually turns over. For example, consider a software retailer. The retailer buys the software (inventory) in batches from a manufacturer and sells them to consumers. As soon as the retailer is able to sell the first batch of software to consumers, the retailer orders another batch of software from the software manufacturer. The faster the retailer is able to sell the batches, the more money it makes and the less amount of time the software has to stay on the shelf. Therefore, higher inventory turnover is good for business. Inventory turnover in Exhibit 21 is worsening. The firm must take steps to reverse the situation.

Profit Performance

A firm can improve revenues by lowering its costs and make profits. Profit performance improvement starts with knowing and understanding the break-even point concept. Break-even point (BEP) occurs where total revenues (TR) equal total costs (TC), meaning the firm makes neither profits nor losses.

TR = TC

When a firm's total revenue (TR) is greater than its total cost (TC), the firm makes profits. On the other hand, when a firm's total costs exceed total revenues, the firm makes losses. Figure 18 illustrates a graphic version of break-even point (BEP). The quantity produced and sold is shown on the horizontal axis. The vertical axis represents revenues, costs, and profits. Break-even point (BEP) occurs where the total costs line intersects the total revenues line or when total costs are equal to total revenues.

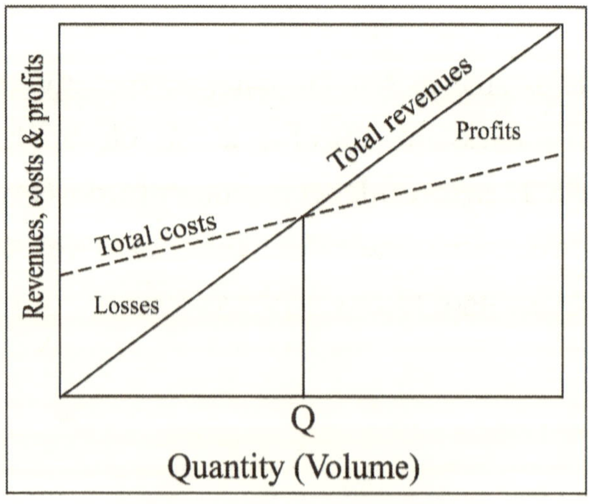

Figure 18: Break-even point

At any point to the right of Q in Figure 18, total revenues (TR) exceed total costs (TC) and the firm makes profits (P). Profits equal total revenues minus total costs.

P = TR - TC

Any point to the left of Q, the firm makes losses since total cost is greater than total revenues. Total cost (TC) consists of fixed costs (FC) plus variable costs (VC).

TC = FC + VC

Fixed costs are costs that remain the same regardless of how much a firm produces and sells. For example, if a firm's rent is $5,000 a month, the firm must meet this rent commitment regardless of the quantity it produces and sells in a month. Variable costs, on the other hand, vary with quantity produced and sold. For example, if a firm increases its production and sales by 20 percent, its variable costs will increase by 20 percent.

Total revenues (TR) equal selling price (SP) of a product multiplied by the quantity (Q) produced and sold.

TR = SP × Q

The formula that follows can be used to calculate a break-even point. UVC represents variable cost per quantity produced. It is obtained by dividing total variable costs by total quantity produced. Break-even point (BEP) is calculated by first subtracting the unit variable cost (UVC) from the selling price (SP) and dividing the result into the total fixed costs (FC).

BEP = FC ÷ [SP – UVC]

The difference between the selling price (SP) and the unit variable cost (UVC) represents the unit contribution margin (UCM). Therefore, unit contribution margin equals selling price minus unit variable cost.

UCM = SP – UVC

The break-even point calculation becomes simply fixed costs divided by the unit contribution margin.

BEP = FC ÷ UCM

The following example will illustrate how to find a break-even point (BEP).

Mini case 1

A firm plans to manufacture a revolutionary computer keyboard. The keyboard, unlike any other, has a scanner, a fax, and a photocopier built into it. The keyboard can scan documents directly into a computer memory. It has the capability to interface with any computer to make changes to documents. This task is possible through the scanning of documents directly into the computer memory.

The firm estimates that fixed costs (FC) are $100,000. Estimated variable costs are $150,000. The firm intends to produce 1,000 keyboards. Unit variable cost (UVC) is $150 per keyboard ($150,000 divided by 1,000 keyboards). The selling price (SP) is $550 per keyboard. The firm wants to find out its break-even point before starting the production of the keyboard for the market.

Solution

BEP = FC ÷ UCM

BEP = $100,000 ÷ [$550 - $150]

BEP = $100,000 ÷ $400

BEP = 250 keyboards

The firm must manufacture and sell 250 keyboards to break even. The firm makes neither profits nor losses with the production and sale of the first 250 keyboards. This represents a break-even point in dollars of $137,500 (250 keyboards times $550 per keyboard).

However, a firm is in business to make profits and not just to break even. A firm must set profit targets. Mini cases 2 and 3 illustrate this.

Mini case 2

The firm wants to know how many computer keyboards it must sell to have profits of $500,000 (desired profit target). The firm faces the same costs and price information as in mini case 1.

Solution

Desired profit before taxes (DPBT) = [Fixed Costs + Profit Target] ÷ UCM

DPBT = ($100,000 + $500,000) ÷ (SP – UVC)

DPBT = $600,000 ÷ ($550 - $150)

DPBT = \$600,000 ÷ \$400

DPBT = 1,500 keyboards

The firm needs to produce and sell 1,500 keyboards in order to achieve its desired profit before-tax of \$500,000.

Mini case 3

The CEO wants to know how many keyboards to manufacture in order to make \$500,000 after tax. The firm faces the same costs and price per keyboard information as before. The firm's tax rate is 40 percent.

Solution

Desired profit after tax (DPAT) = Fixed Cost + [Profit Target ÷ (1 - tax rate)] ÷ UCM

DPAT = [\$100,000 + Profit Target ÷ (1 - tax rate)] ÷ UCM

DPAT = [\$100,000 + [\$500,000 ÷ (1 - 0.40)]] ÷ UCM

DPAT = [\$100,000 + [\$500,000 ÷ 0.60]] ÷ \$400

DPAT = [\$100,000 + \$833,333] ÷ \$400

DPAT = \$933,333 ÷ \$400

DPAT = 2,334 keyboards.

The firm must produce 2,334 keyboards in order to meet the desired profit after tax target of \$500,000.

The calculation of the break-even point is a starting point that allows the firm to pursue one or more of the following approaches to improve profit performance:

- Produce and sell more above break-even quantity
- Increase selling price
- Increase unit contribution margin
- Decrease fixed costs
- Decrease variable costs

Strategy Attractiveness Measures (SAM)

There are several ways to evaluate or measure the attractiveness of a business strategy. The techniques range from simple to complex. The aim of business strategy is to make a firm better off than it used to be. A decision to pursue a course of action makes sense only if it improves the well-being of the firm and its shareholders. If a strategy puts a business in a compromising position and makes the firm worse off, the strategy is not worth pursuing. More importantly, a great deal of thought should go into determining whether the benefit of a particular strategy is greater than the cost of pursuing that strategy. As a result, business strategy proposals must be evaluated as to their attractiveness. Some of the techniques for evaluating the attractiveness of a business strategy are:

- Payback period method
- Net present value (NPV) method
- Profitability index (PI) method

Mini case

To illustrate each method, consider a firm that is under competitive pressure. The CEO along with other senior management decide that the only way out of the competitive pressures is to develop a new product that would reverse the aging process of humans without a need for cosmetic surgery. The firm's market research indicates that the product would receive very high consumer acceptance.

The firm, being the first on the market, will command a substantial monopoly power and market share. Business intelligence information presented to the CEO shows that it would be ahead of other competitors in the industry for at least five years. If competitors succeeded in developing a similar product, the CEO would commit resources to develop and market a new product that would perform even better. In this way, the competitors would be playing catch-up all the time.

After a lengthy and tedious strategy meeting, the CEO identifies Canada as an excellent place to market the product. The initial cash outflow would be $15 million. This amount will come from loans from a financial institution. Interest charges on the loans will be at 10 percent interest per year. The cash inflow for the next five years would be $5 million each year. The CEO wants to know if marketing the product in Canada makes economic sense.

Solution

a) Payback Method

A payback method shows the number of years and months it takes to repay the initial investment (initial cash outlay) in the project. In this case, the payback method shows that the firm would be able to repay the full $15 million it borrowed from the bank in three years.

When the amounts of cash inflow from a project are equal each year, the firm must calculate the payback period by simply dividing the initial cash outlay (initial investment in the project) by the annual cash inflow. In this particular case, divide $15 million by $5 million to obtain a payback period of three years. The three years represent the length of time it will take the firm to repay the $15 million.

Payback period = Initial cash outlay ÷ annual cash inflow

= $15 million ÷ $5 million

= 3 years

The payback period method can be challenging to estimate when the annual cash inflows are not equal. Let us say the yearly cash inflows are as follows:

Year 1: $1 million

Year 2: $2 million

Year 3: $3 million

Year 4: $5 million

Year 5: $8 million

Unlike the previous example, the amounts received (cash inflow) from the project are not the same each year. The simplest and fastest way to estimate the payback is to assume that the amounts received from the project each year go towards repaying the $15 million borrowed from the bank. The amounts received from the project, starting from Year 1 through Year 4 ($1million + $2 million + $3 million + $5 million), equal $11 million. This means that at the end of Year 4, the firm could repay $11 million to the financial institution. It would still owe $4 million to the financial institution. The firm could repay the remaining amount between the end of Year 4 and the end of Year 5.

Since the full $15 million would not have been recovered in Year 4, with $4 million remaining ($15million - $11 million), to estimate the length of time it would take to repay the remaining $4 million, divide the remaining $4 million by $8 million to be received in Year 5 ($4 million ÷ $8 million). The result is 6 months or half a year. Therefore, the payback period for this uneven cash flow is four years and six months. This represents the length of time it would take the firm to repay the full $15 million to the financial institution.

With this information, the CEO can decide if four years and six months is a reasonable length of time to repay the initial investments in the project. This information will affect the CEO's decision to market the product in Canada.

The payback method provides an indication of the financial attractiveness of the strategy project in question.

b) Net Present Value (NPV) Method

The net present value is equal to the difference between the discounted cash flow expected from a project (strategy project in our case) and the initial cash outlay (initial investment) in the project. The criteria for judging the attractiveness of a strategy project is that the discounted cash flow expected from the project must be more than the initial cash investment in the project. If the discounted cash flow from the project were less than the initial cash investment, then it would make no economic sense to pursue the strategy from the point of view of NPV. This simply means that a strategy project that has a positive net present value (NPV) is good for the firm. On the other hand, a negative NPV from a project reduces the value and profitability of a firm. A strategy project is attractive if it has a positive NPV. On the other hand, a strategy project is unattractive if its NPV is negative.

The net present value focuses on time value of money. Time value of money refers to how much a dollar received today is worth compared to how much the same dollar would be worth if it were to be received sometime in the future. According to the time value of money, a dollar received today is worth more than a dollar in some distant future. The reason is that a dollar in the hand today can be invested today and earn interest now, whereas money promised but not received until some future date loses the opportunity to earn interest today.

The NPV calculation is not as simple as its definition appears. In this case, the firm would expect to receive $5 million every year for the next five years. This money is the cash flow from the strategy project. The next consideration in the calculation of the NPV is discount rate. The discount rate represents the cost (interest cost) of borrowing money from a financial institution or the rate at which money would earn interest if invested.

The discount factor from a present value annuity table at a 10 percent interest rate is 3.791. It is easier to calculate the NPV when the cash flow amount is the same every year. In that case, multiply the annual cash flow of $5 million by 3.791 first to obtain a discounted cash flow (DCF), then subtract the initial $15 million cash outflow (initial investment) from the discounted cash flow (DCF) to obtain the NPV.

DCF = $5,000,000 × 3.791

DCF = $18,955,000

Since the initial investment is $15,000,000, deduct this amount from the $18,955,000 to obtain the NPV.

NPV = $18,955,000 - $15,000,000

NPV = $3,955,000

Since the NPV is positive, everything being equal, the CEO should approve the project to market the product in Canada. It is an attractive strategy project.

c) Profitability Index Method (PIM)

Profitability index (PI) is a cost-benefit ratio, which focuses on the discounted cash flow (DCF) divided by the initial cash outlay (investment) for the strategy project. The criteria for judging the attractiveness of a strategy project using the profitability index (PI) is to have a PI that is greater than or equal to one. A strategy project that has a PI of less than 1.0 is normally rejected. The PI in this case is calculated by taking the DCF, $18,955,000, divided by the initial cash outflow of $15 million, resulting in a PI of 1.26.

Profitability Index (PI) = DCF ÷ initial cash outflow (investment)

= $18,955,000 ÷ $15,000,000

PI = 1.26

The profitability index (PI) of 1.26 indicates that the benefits outweigh the cost of pursuing the strategy. Since the PI is greater than 1.0, the CEO would accept the project and approve the product to be marketed in Canada. The strategy project is attractive.

Chapter 8

Strategy Decision Tree

A strategy decision tree (SDT) is a systematic and sequential process for evaluating decisions involving risks and uncertainties. A strategy decision tree is constructed by using a square to represent a starting point of a decision. A circle represents an outcome or the result of a decision. Probabilities are used to represent risks associated with the outcomes of decisions.

Steps for developing a strategy decision tree (SDT) are:

Step 1: Identify the main alternatives on which decision is required.

Step 2: Draw a square to represent the starting point of the decision.

Step 3: Draw an oblique line pointing upwards to the right from the square.

Step 4: Draw another oblique line pointing downwards to the right from the square.

Step 5: Draw a square at the end of the top oblique line and at the end of the bottom oblique line to represent decisions points.

Step 6: If there are no more decisions to be made, draw a small circle at the end of each line (branch).

Step 7: Write the dollar value of the anticipated revenue outcome (ARO) beside each small circle.

Step 8: Write the probabilities associated with each outcome on the outcome branches. The sum of all the probabilities assigned to the branches originating from each square must add up to 1.0.

Mini case

Wincor is an imaginary Canadian firm located in the province of Ontario. The firm retails construction materials and related supplies similar to those that Home Depot offers. The chief executive officer is looking for an opportunity to grow in domestic and foreign markets. The CEO knows all too well about the risks involved in expanding into these markets. A systematic assessment of the different courses of action and the risks associated with them will allow the CEO to make a final decision about the growth strategy. The CEO asks for a strategy decision tree to be prepared prior to making a final decision. The firm has to decide whether to expand in the domestic markets or in the foreign markets. The choices of foreign markets are the United States of America (USA), China, and India. The domestic markets under consideration are three provinces in Canada — Ontario, Alberta, and Quebec.

The objective for expanding into new markets is to increase the firm's profits and growth. The firm will base its decision on which of the alternative markets would yield profits greater than $200,000.

Exhibit 22 summarizes the costs for expanding into foreign and domestic markets; which include costs related to warehouse construction, labour, advertising, marketing, staff training, and so on. For example, the cost to expand into the USA and Ontario are $83,500 and $90,000 respectively. Interpret the rest of Exhibit 22 in the same manner.

Exhibit 22: Market expansion costs			
Foreign markets	**Cost**	**Domestic markets**	**Cost**
USA	$83,500	Ontario (Canada)	$90,000
China	$72,000	Alberta (Canada)	$70,000
India	$9,000	Quebec (Canada)	$60,000

Exhibit 23 shows the revenues from the markets under different economic assumptions. The risk or probabilities associated with different economic growth assumptions are in brackets.

For example, in Exhibit 23 when the economic growth condition in the USA is high, the firm makes $350,000. On the other hand, if the economic growth conditions in the USA were medium or low, revenues are $35,000 or $15,000 respectively. Interpret the rest of Exhibit 23 in the same manner.

Exhibit 23: Anticipated revenue outcomes (ARO) for domestic and foreign markets						
Economic growth	**USA**	**China**	**India**	**Ontario**	**Alberta**	**Quebec**
High	$350,000 (0.5)	$500,000 (0.3)	$400,000 (0.1)	$400,000 (0.1)	$300,000 (0.3)	$300,000 (0.3)
Medium	$35,000 (0.3)	$40,000 (0.2)	$20,000 (0.3)	$30,000 (0.6)	$200,000 (0.1)	$20,000 (0.6)
Low	$15,000 (0.2)	$8,000 (0.5)	$5,000 (0.6)	$10,000 (0.3)	$100,000 (0.6)	$5,000 (0.1)

Solution

Figure 19: Strategy Decision Tree

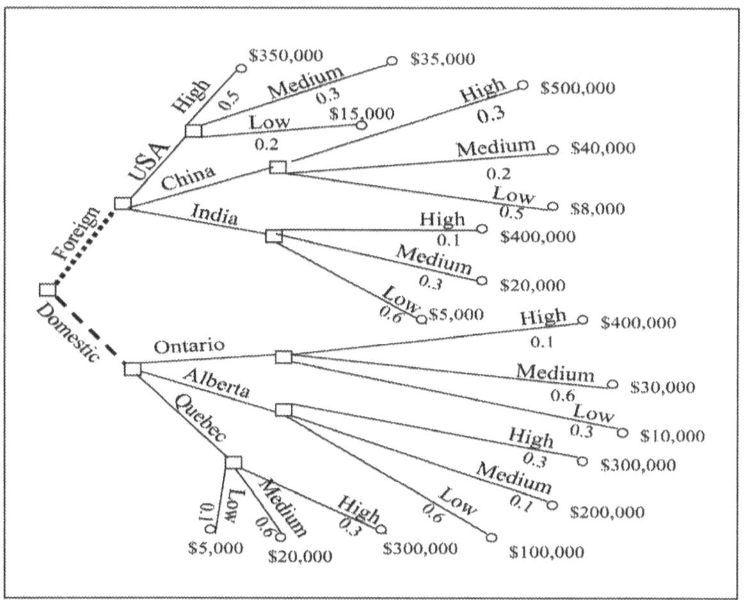

Figure 19 shows a strategy decision tree for the foreign market entry and domestic market entry. The calculations and the expected monetary value for each market are as shown in Exhibit 24.

The construction of the decision tree shown in Figure 19 is based on the information from Exhibit 23. Exhibit 24 shows how to calculate the expected monetary values (EMV) from each market using the information from the decision tree. The EMV is simply a product of the revenues from the markets and the respective probabilities (or risk). For example, the EMV for the Ontario market in a period of high economic growth is $400,000 x 0.1, which is equal to an EMV of $40,000. To obtain the total EMV, add all the EMVs for each market in the columns. For example, the total EMV for China is $162,000 ($150,000 + $8,000 + $4,000).

Exhibit 24: Expected monetary value calculations for domestic and foreign markets						
Economic growth	**USA**	**China**	**India**	**Ontario**	**Alberta**	**Quebec**
High	$350,000 × 0.5 EMV = $175,000	$500,000 × 0.3 EMV = $150,000	$400,000 × 0.1 EMV = $40,000	$400,000 × 0.1 EMV = $40,000	$300,000 × 0.3 EMV = $90,000	$300,000 × 0.3 EMV = $90,000
Medium	$35,000 × 0.3 EMV = $10,500	$40,000 × 0.2 EMV = $8,000	$20,000 × 0.3 EMV = $6,000	$30,000 × 0.6 EMV = $18,000	$200,000 × 0.1 EMV = $20,000	$20,000 × 0.6 EMV = $12,000
Low	$15,000 × 0.2 EMV = $3,000	$8,000 × 0.5 EMV = $4,000	$5,000 × 0.6 EMV = $3,000	$10,000 × 0.3 EMV = $3,000	$100,000 × 0.6 EMV = $60,000	$5,000 × 0.1 EMV = $500
Total EMV	**$188,500**	**$162,000**	**$49,000**	**$61,000**	**$170,000**	**$102,500**

Exhibit 25 is a summary of the expected monetary values (EMV) and costs associated with entering each market. The last row of Exhibit 25 shows the net expected monetary value (NEMV) after subtracting the costs from the total expected values.

Exhibit 25: Summary of expected monetary values (EMV) and costs						
	USA	**China**	**India**	**Ontario**	**Alberta**	**Quebec**
Total EMV (from Exhibit 24)	$188,500	$162,000	$49,000	$61,000	$170,000	$102,500
Cost (from Exhibit 22)	-$83,000	-$72,000	-$9,000	-$90,000	-$70,000	-$60,000
Net expected monetary value (NEMV)	**$105,500**	**$90,000**	**$40,000**	**-$29,000**	**$100,000**	**$42,500**

In order to decide if the firm should expand into the three foreign markets or expand in the three domestic markets, it is necessary to first add all the net expected monetary values

(NEMV) from the foreign markets together and then add all the net expected monetary values (NEMV) from the domestic markets together. This results in revenues of $235,500 (consisting of U.S.A: $105,500; China: $90,000; and India: $40,000) for the foreign markets and $113,500 (comprised of Ontario: $-29,000; Alberta: $100,000; and Quebec: $42,500) for the domestic markets. Everything being equal, the CEO should grow into the foreign markets now. The three foreign markets together are more attractive than all the three domestic markets combined.

PART IV

Strategy Management

Chapter 9

Strategy Project Management

Business strategy requires resources and time commitments to develop and implement. A firm achieves success through its ability to meet its desired goals. This means that a firm must manage strategy as if it were a project. A project management approach to business strategy has many benefits including:

- Better control of the strategy formulation through to implementation
- More focus on costs to avoid cost over-runs
- Sharper orientation towards strategy goals
- Better control over strategy outcomes
- Shorter cycle times for the strategy
- Opportunity to motivate people towards strategy goals
- Better coordination and control of activities, budgets, equipment, and resources
- Better response to the changing environment
- Sharper and quicker decision-making
- Better and faster strategy results

Strategy project management must meet cost, time, quality, and performance objectives as shown in Figure 20. Proper management of business strategy formulation through to implementation (execution) will ensure that a business strategy will fall within budget, be completed on time, and will meet quality and performance objectives.

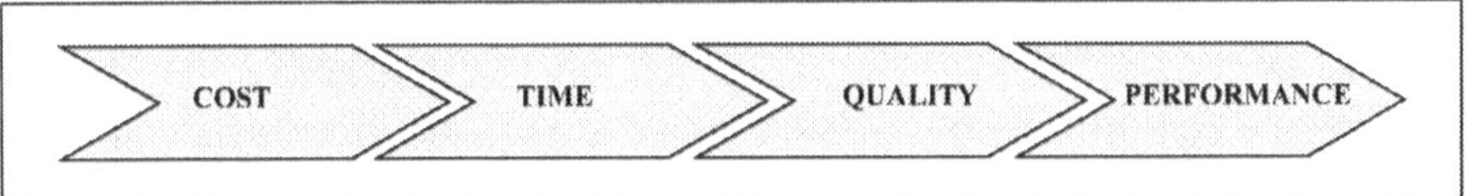

Figure 20: Project Performance Objectives

Planning, budgeting, resource allocation and scheduling must accompany business strategy formulation through to implementation. Furthermore, managing resources such as people, equipment, funds, and material is important in ensuring that the business strategy project will meet its desired objectives.

Business strategy has a short and a small window of opportunity. Competitors can easily catch up with whatever other firms come up with; whether this involves a merger, new product development, cost focus, or a differentiation strategy.

A strategy project must go through phases as shown in Figure 21. During the strategy formulation phase, the firm's management discusses ideas on how the firm would compete. The strategy selection phase refers to the stage where the firm decides on the criteria for selecting a particular course of action. The net present value, payback, or profitability index may form part of the strategy selection criteria.

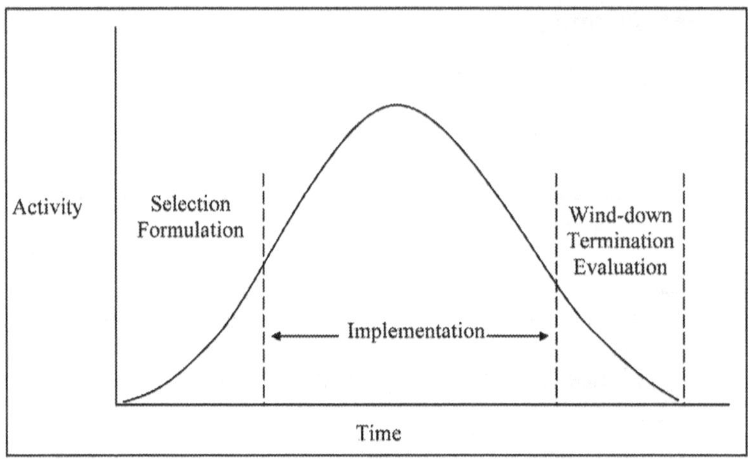

Figure 21: Strategy Project Phases

The strategy implementation phase involves taking action. Other phases are the strategy wind-down phase, strategy termination phase, and strategy evaluation phase. The strategy evaluation phase involves identifying lessons learned, such as what went well and what needs improving the next time around.

A strategy project must have an implementation plan. The content of the strategy implementation plan must include:

- Purpose and scope of the strategy project
- The objectives and goals of the strategy project
- Break down of tasks or work to be accomplished
- Assignment of responsibilities to each activity or task
- The start and finish time for each task
- Allocation of resources to each task or activity
- The monitoring and control system for the strategy project

- Identification and management of risks associated with the strategy project
- Communications and project management

Figure 22 shows examples of elements to include in a strategy project plan.

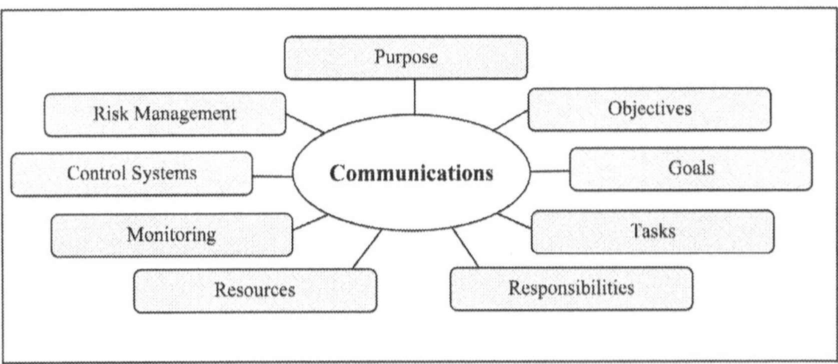

Figure 22: Strategy Project Plan

Planning for strategy formulation through to implementation can contribute greatly to the attainment of the strategy project objectives. Recruiting, managing, and motivating the project team are critical to the success of the strategy project. While planning does not guarantee that a business strategy will meet its predetermined objectives, it beats a helter-skelter approach to strategy formulation and implementation.

Chapter 10

Strategy Risk Management (SRM)

Strategy risk management involves managing risks associated with business strategy by taking proactive and preventive measures to identify and deal with risks before they actually occur. This allows decisions to focus on what could materially affect the successful execution and outcomes of a strategy. Risk management is not a one-time activity. The formulation, execution, and termination of a business strategy must take into account or integrate risk management.

Managing strategy project risks has many benefits. It allows strategy decision-makers to move away from firefighting, chaos, and crisis management to a situation where risks are managed in a more proactive, systematic, and preventive manner.

Many sources of risks exist today which include:

- Financial risks
- Market risks
- Operational risks
- Legal liability risks
- Political risks
- Business risks
- Economic risks
- Social risks

- Technological risks
- Environmental risks

Other forms of risk, which are global in nature, may include:

- Terrorism risks
- Risks of pandemics
- Risk of natural disasters

Virtually anything that has the potential of preventing a business strategy from achieving its desired objectives is a risk. It is important therefore to have a systematic way to identify and incorporate risk management routinely into the formulation and implementation of a business strategy project.

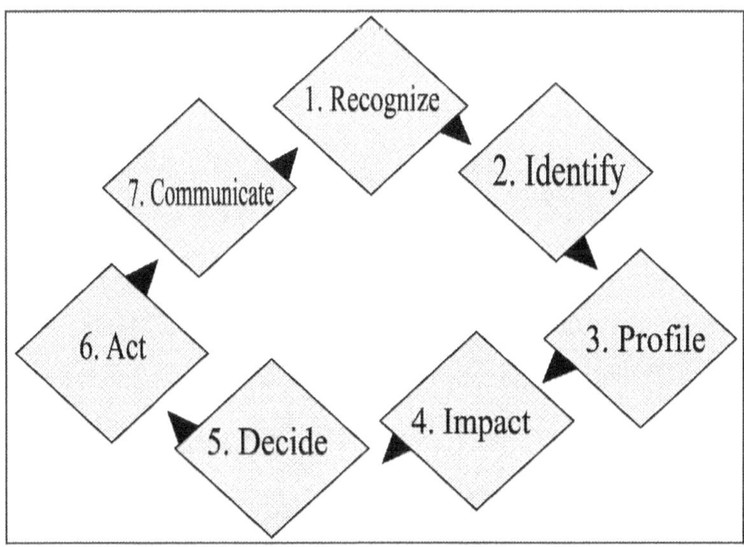

Figure 23: Strategy Risk Management Cycle

Figure 23 shows a systematic way to manage risk, which includes:

- Recognizing that risks exist
- Identifying the risks
- Developing a risk profile using ranking
- Assessing the impact of risks
- Making decisions about the risks
- Taking action to deal with risks
- Communicating risks

The first phase in risk management is to recognize that there are risks that can negatively affect the results of a business strategy. The second stage is to identify all the possible things that can go wrong with the business strategy. Some of the things that negatively affect a business strategy include technological risk, legal risks, economic risk, financial risk, market risks, risk of natural disasters, and so on.

Next, it is important to rank the risks as to their importance, that is, how much of the firm's attention each deserves. After ranking the risks, decision-makers must assess the likelihood of the risk occurring and their level of impact. Then, decisions have to be made about the risks, action must be taken to deal with them, and the risks must be communicated.

Actions to take are shown in Figure 24 and include:

- Reducing risk
- Mitigating risk
- Monitoring risk
- Controlling risk
- Eliminating risk
- Avoiding risk
- Accepting risk

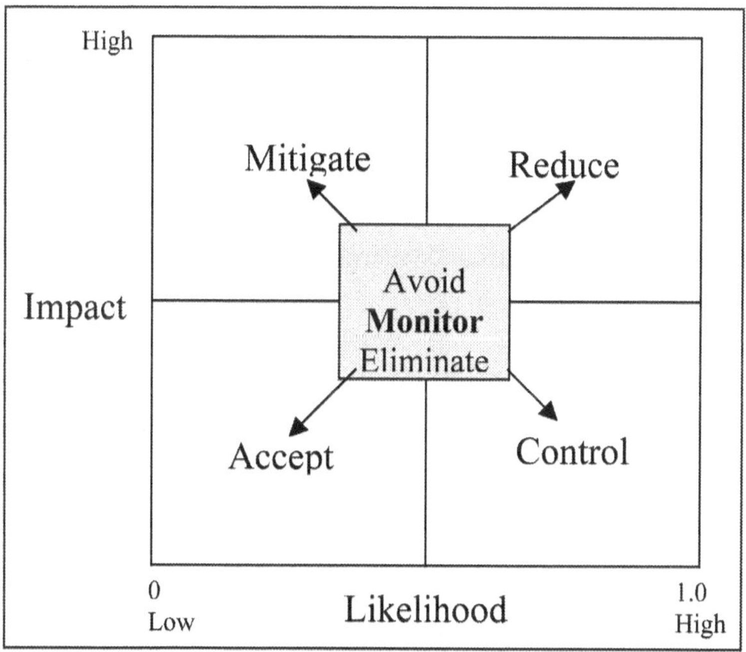

Figure 24: Strategy Risk Management

Chapter 11

The Strategy Roadmap

A business strategy is about achieving better and faster results. It must take into account what is happening now and what is to happen in the future. A firm's strategy must have clear and well-articulated objectives. The objectives, for example, can be to achieve better and faster overall performance, higher profitability, better growth or increased market share. An effective business strategy aims at making a firm more viable and attractive to investors and stakeholders. Continued viability of a firm depends on a business strategy that brings about positive and successful results more quickly. In order to achieve the desired objectives, managers and executives must master the secrets of business strategy.

At this point, you have acquired a great deal of knowledge, skills, and understanding required for developing an effective business strategy for your firm. As a final stage in the development of a strategy mindset and a visual map, the sections in this chapter provide a clear, simpler, and innovative roadmap for developing a business strategy for achieving better and faster results. Business strategy development has never been simpler than what this book offers. Everything you need to develop a business strategy is found in one place as shown in Figure 26. There is no longer the need to search in many places for what you need for developing a business strategy. Figure 26 provides a one-stop shop for a business strategy.

The Strategy Navigator (SN) in Figure 25 is conceptual in nature and gives firms the bigger picture and a mental map of what needs to be considered when developing a strategy. The Strategy Roadmap (SR) shown in Figure 26 on the other hand is more practical and walks executives, managers, and business owners through the phases and the components to consider when developing an effective strategy for their organization. The Strategy Navigator and the Strategy Roadmap are the focus of this chapter.

Today, managers and executives are under constant pressure to produce better and faster results to improve performance. They must not only respond to the ever-changing business challenges, but also act faster and in a more proactive manner. Opportunities are short-lived. Business strategy has a short window of opportunity to make a difference. Failure to respond to challenges and threats, missing opportunities, or acting too late or in the wrong way can cause an organization many undue hardships. Organizations must seize opportunities, minimize or eliminate threats, turn weaknesses into strengths, and capitalize on strengths. This must be done with speed and agility in order to achieve better and faster results. It is of little use to have a strategy that takes too long to develop and implement. In order to realize its ultimate results, the development of a business strategy must use a surgical and systematic approach. The Strategy

Roadmap (SR) and the Strategy Navigator (SN) tie together the tools and the models discussed in the previous chapters and offer you a systematic and a visual map that you can apply immediately to develop an effective strategy.

Strategy Navigator (SN)

As illustrated in Figure 25, a business strategy must be compatible with the vision and mission of the organization. The strategy must be consistent with management beliefs, and the values of the organization. For example, it would be an uphill battle for an organization to make a radical change to improve the overall performance when its management team is very conservative, pessimistic, and risk averse.

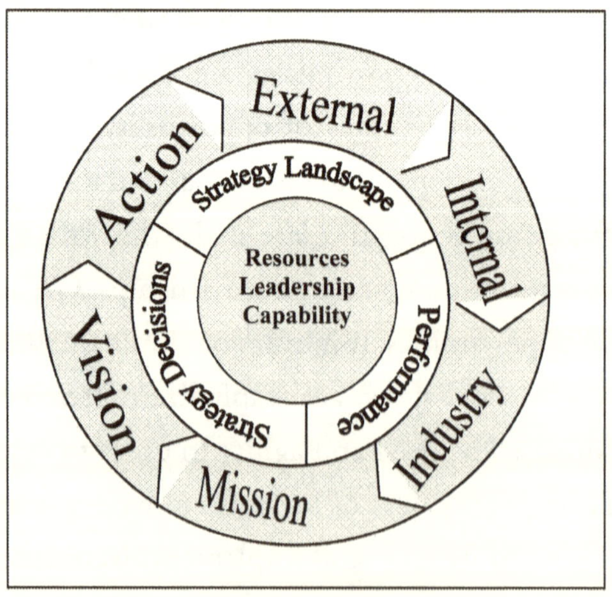

Figure 25: Strategy Navigator (SN)

Furthermore, all the pieces of a business strategy must fit together. If they do not fit, the firm must abandon the strategy or alter it. This may be necessary, especially if the strategy is at odds with the current management beliefs and capabilities.

Strategy Roadmap (SR)

The SR uses a project approach that walks the decision-maker through the steps involved in developing a business strategy for your firm. Each step consists of elements or components. This provides the decision-maker with a structure and a method for strategy development. In reality, the process of strategy development through to implementation is not always a straight line. It does not have to precisely follow a prescribed pattern, starting with step one and ending with the last step. The Strategy Roadmap is a guidance system. It provides a visual and mental map for decision-makers to develop a business strategy and achieve better and faster results.

The SR is not a rigid process for developing and implementing strategy. It is an "out of the box" guide for applying creativity, flexibility, ingenuity, and innovation in developing a business strategy. In the changing and dynamic competitive world of business, nothing stands still. The use of the SR can be as robust as the decision-maker wants it to be. In certain situations, only certain elements may be important to a firm, given its individual and unique business circumstances.

The major benefit of the Strategy Roadmap is that it provides those responsible for strategy with an at-a-glance "telescopic view" of the phases and their components that must be considered for developing an effective business strategy. This allows each firm to select components and develop a business strategy that is different and unique.

The Strategy Roadmap (SR) brings everything together like a jigsaw puzzle. The SR is simple and helps to develop a strategy mindset in executives and business owners. By breaking strategy into different phases, it makes it simpler to develop a strategy for better and faster results.

The Strategy Roadmap consists of:

Phase 1: Strategy mission
Phase 2: External environment
Phase 3: Industry environment
Phase 4: Internal environment
Phase 5: Strategy landscape
Phase 6: Strategy decisions
Phase 7: Performance measures
Phase 8: Strategy action

Figure 26: Strategy Roadmap (SR)

Strategy Mission →	External Environment →	Industry Environment →	Internal Environment →	Strategy Landscape →	Strategy Decisions →	Performance Measures →	Strategy Action
• Strategy drivers • Purpose • Vision • Values • Objective • Goals • Strategy fit	• Global • Social • Technological • Political • Legal • Economic • Demographic • Government • Ecological	• PIE model • S-C-P model • Market structure • Direct competitor map • Business intelligence	• SWOT • SWOT profile • PVCS model • Market segmentation • Segmentation variables • Market share • Relative market share • ARC framework • Business blind spots • Competitive advantage • SCA	• Strategy types • ACID strategy • Cost strategy • Pricing strategy • Differentiation strategy • Positioning strategy • Growth strategy • Resource-based strategy • Business combination strategy • Cooperation strategy	• Decisions under certainty • Decisions under risk • Decisions under uncertainty • Management decisions • Strategy decision tree	• Financial performance • Financial condition ratios • Investment utilization ratios • Profitability ratios • Overall performance ratios • Break-even point • Payback method • Net present value • Profitability index	• Strategy project management • Strategy risk management • Strategy management • Management commitment • Leadership

Figure 26 brings all the pieces needed to develop an effective strategy for better and faster results together in one place. In addition to the phases in Figure 26, these questions will guide decision-makers in developing their respective strategy.

- How does each of the components affect your firm now and in the future?
- What can your firm do to diminish or eliminate negative impacts?
- What opportunities in the environment can your firm capitalize on?
- Does your firm have enough resources and capabilities to deal with threats and opportunities?
- How can your firm dominate its market or industry?
- In what type of market does your firm operate?
- How can your firm earn above-normal profits or above-average returns?
- What activities should your firm start doing, stop doing, or continue doing?
- How can your firm turn its weaknesses into strengths, capitalize on strengths, eliminate or minimize threats and weaknesses, and capitalize on opportunities?
- What is the appropriate strategy to deploy?
- Are your firm's mission, vision, values, and management beliefs consistent with the chosen strategy?

- Does your firm have sufficient resources and capabilities to compete?
- How can your firm increase profitability, market share, growth, or overall performance?

This concludes the journey into the world of business strategy. It is hoped that this book has enhanced your knowledge and understanding of business strategy and that your strategy mindset and visual map will continue to guide you towards achieving better and faster results for your organization.

Reference

Aaker, David A., V. Kumar, and George S. Day. Marketing research, 5th edition. John Wiley & Sons, Inc., 1995.

Andrew, K. The concept of corporate strategy. Richard D. Irwin: Homewood IL., 1971.

Anthony, Robert N., James S. Reece, and Julie Hertenstein. Accounting: Text and cases, 9th edition. Richard D. Irwin Inc., 1994.

Armit, R., and P. Shoemaker. Strategic assets and organizational rent. Strategic Management Journal, January, 1993.

Baldwin, John R., and Joanne Johnson. Business strategies in innovation and non-innovative firms in Canada. Statistics Canada. Catalogue no. 11F0019MPE No. 73, 1995.

Baldwin, John R. Innovation: The key to success in small firms. Statistics Canada. Catalogue no. 11F0019MPE No. 76, 1995.

Barney, Jay B. Firm resources and sustained competitive advantage. Journal of Management, 17 (March), 1991.

Barney, Jay B. Gaining and sustaining competitive advantage, 2nd edition. Pearson Education, Inc., 2002.

Barney, Jay B. Strategic factor markets: Expenditure, luck and business strategy. Management Science 32 (October), 1986

Baye, Michael R. Managerial economics and business strategy, 3rd edition. The McGraw-Hill Companies, Inc., 2000.

Beamish, Paul W., and C. Patrick Woodcock. Strategic management: Text, readings, and cases, 5th edition. McGraw-Hill Ryerson Limited, 1999.

Beckman, Dale M., John M. Rigby. Foundations of marketing, 7th Canadian edition. Harcourt Canada Ltd., 2001.

Bergeron, Pierre G. Finance for non-financial managers, 4th edition. Nelson, 2004.

Bized. The Music Industry: Facing new challenges? www.bized.ac.uk/research/ 2003_04/011203.htm

Boame, Atta K., and Denis Poulin. Mad cow disease and beef trade. Statistics Canada. Catalogue no. 11-621-MIE-No. 005, 2003.

Boame, Atta K., William Parson, and Michael Trant. Mad cow disease and beef trade: An update. Statistics Canada. Catalogue no. 11-621-MIE-No. 010, 2004.

Bourgeois, L.J III, and D.R Brodwin. Strategic implementation: Five approaches to an elusive phenomenon. Strategic Management Journal, 5, 1984.

Brennan, T. Five economic indicators you should watch. http://www.forbes.com/strategies/2005/02/04/cx_tdb_0204indicators.html

Buzzell, R.D., Bradley T. Gale, and R.G.M Sultan. Market share – a key to profitability. Harvard Business Review, 53, 1975.

Buzzell, R.D., and Bradley T. Gale. The PIMS principle: Linking strategy to performance. New York: The Free Press, 1987.

Carlton, Dennis W., and Jeffrey M. Perloff. Modern industrial organization. Harper Collins Publishers, 1990.

Caves, R. Industrial organization, corporate strategy and structure. Journal of Economic Literature 18, 1980.

Chandler, A.D. Jr., Strategy and structure. Garden City, N.Y: Doubleday, 1962.

CIPO. A guide to copy rights. Canadian Intellectual Property Office, September 2003. Cat. No. RG 43-27/2003E.

CIPO. A guide to trade-marks. Canadian Intellectual Property Office, September 2002. Cat. No. RG 43-32/2002E.

CIPO. A guide to patents. Canadian Intellectual Property Office, September 2002. Cat. No. RG 43-33/2002E.

CIPO. A guide to industrial designs. Canadian Intellectual Property Office, January 2002. Cat. No. RG 43-28/2001E.

Collis, David J., and Cynthia A. Montgomery. Competing on resources: Strategy in the 1990s. Harvard Business Review, 73 (July-August), 1995.

Cool, Karel, and Dan Schendel. Performance differences among strategic group members. Strategic Management Journal, 9 (May-June), 1988.

Cool, Karel, and Dan Schendel. Strategic group formation and performance: The case of the US pharmaceutical industry, 1970-84. Management Science, 33, 1987.

Cravens, David W., Charles W. Lamb Jr., and Victoria L. Crittenden. Strategic marketing management cases, 6th edition. The McGraw-Hill Companies Inc., 1999.

Day, G., and R. Wensley. Assessing advantages: A framework for diagnosing competitive superiority. Journal of Marketing, 52, 1988.

Dierckx, I., and K. Cool. Asset stock accumulation and sustainability of competitive advantage. Management Science, 35, 1989.

Eisenhardt, K.M., and J.A Martin. Dynamic capabilities: What are they? Strategic Management Journal, 52, 2000.

Eisenhardt, K.M. Making fast strategic decisions in high velocity environments. Academy of Management Journal, 32, 1998.

Eisenhardt, K.M., and M.J Zbaracki. Strategic decision making. Strategic Management Journal, 13, 1992.

Faulkner, David, and Cliff Bowman. The essence of competitive strategy. Prentice-Hall International (UK) Limited, 1995.

Federal Reserve Bank of New York. Economic Indicators (By the numbers). http://www.newyorkfed.org/education/bythe.html

Fiegenbaum, A., and H. Thomas. Strategic group and performance: The US insurance industry. Strategic Management Journal, 8, 1990.

Financial ratios and quality indicators. www.onlinewbc.gov/docs/finance/fs_ratio1.html

Freiberg, K., J. Freiberg. Nuts!: Southwest Airlines crazy recipe for business and personal success. Bard Press: Austin, 1996.

Fry, Joseph N. and J. Peter Killing. Strategic analysis and action, 3rd edition. Prentice-Hall Canada Inc., 1995.

Fuch, Peter H., Kenneth E. Mifflin, Danny Miller, and John O. Whitney. Strategic integration: Competing in the age of capabilities. California Management Review, Spring 2000.

Garrison, Ray H. Managerial accounting, 3rd edition. Business Publications Inc., 1982.

Ghemawat, Pankaj, and Daniel Levinthal. Choice structures. Business strategy and performance: A generalized NK-simulation approach. WP 00-05. The Wharton School, University of Pennsylvania, November 1999 and May 2000.

Ghemawat, Pankaj. Competition and business strategy in historical perspective. Harvard Business School Press: Boston MA, HBSP # 798-010, 1998.

Ghemawat, Pankaj. Commitment: The dynamic of strategy. New York: The Free Press, 1991.

Ghemawat, Pankaj. Strategy and the business landscape. Addison-Wesley, 1999.

Gibbins, Michael. Financial accounting: An integrated approach, 2nd edition. Nelson Canada, 1995.

Gilad, Benjamin. Business blindspots. Probus Publishing Company, 1994.

Gittell, J.H. Coordinating service across functional boundaries: The departure process at Southwest Airlines. Harvard Business School working paper no. 98-050, 1998.

Gluck, F.W., and S.P Kaufman, and A.S Walleck. The four phases of strategic management. The Journal of Business Strategy, 1982.

Golden, B.R. SBU strategy and performance: The moderating effects of the corporate-SBU relationship. Strategic Management Journal, 13, 1992.

Granof, Michael H., Financial accounting: Principles and issues. Prentice-Hall, Inc., 1997.

Grant, R.M. Contemporary strategy analysis, 3rd edition. Blackwell, 1998.

Grant, R.M. The resource-based theory of competitive advantage: Implications for strategy formulation. California Management Review, Spring 1991.

Gupta, A.K. SBU strategies, corporate-SBU relations, and SBU effectiveness in strategy implementation. Academy of Management Journal, 30, 1987.

Gupta, A.K., and V. Govindarajan. Business unit strategy, managerial characteristics, and business unit effectiveness at strategy implementation. Academy of Management Journal, 27, 1987.

Hambrick, D.C., I.C MacMillan, and D.L Day. Strategic attributes and performance in BCG matrix – a PIMS-based analysis. Academy of Management Review, 25, 1982.

Hamel, G., and C.K Prahalad. Competing for the future. Harvard Business Review, 1994.

Hamel, G., and C.K Prahalad. Strategic intent. Harvard Business Review, 1989.

Harrigan, K.R. Strategy formulation in declining industries. Academy of Management Review, 5, 1980.

Henderson, Bruce D. The origin of strategy. Harvard Business Review, November–December 1989.

Hill, C.W.L. Differentiation versus low cost or differentiation and low cost: A contingency framework. Academy of Management Review, 13, 1988.

Industry Canada. Industrial intelligence (Biotechnology Sector). Life Sciences Branch, 2004.

Industry Canada. Industrial intelligence (Steel Sector). Manufacturing Industries Branch, 2004.

Industry Canada. Industrial intelligence profile (Oil and Gas Equipment and Services Sector). Energy and Marine Branch, 2004.

International Federation of the Phonographic Industry (IFPI) What is piracy? http://www.ifpi.org

Investor Guide.Com. Economic indicators http://investorguide.com/igueconindicator.html

Jacobsen, R. The persistence of abnormal returns. Strategic Management Journal, 9, 1988.

Johnson, G., and K. Scholes. Exploring corporate strategy, 3rd edition, Prentice-Hall, Hemel Hempstead, 1993.

Kaplan, R., and D. Norton. Putting the balanced scorecard to work, Harvard Business Review, September-October, 1993.

Karnani, A. Generic competitive strategies – Analytical approach. Strategic Management Journal, 5, 1984.

Kay, John. The structure of strategy. Business Strategy Review, 1993.

Keller, Gerald, and Brian Warrack. Statistics for management and economics, 4th edition. Duxbury Press, 1997.

Koch, Richard, The financial times guide to strategy, 2nd edition. Prentice-Hall, 2000.

Koch, Richard. Smart things to know about strategy. Capstone Publishing Limited, 1999.

Kotler, Philip, Peggy H. Cunningham, and Ronald E. Turner. Marketing management. Canadian 10th edition. Pearson Education Canada Inc., 2001.

Lewis, Pam, and Howard Thomas. The linkage between strategy, strategic groups and performance in U.K retail grocery industry. Strategic Management Journal, September, 1990.

Lewis, Jordan D. Partnerships for profits: Structuring and managing strategic alliances. The Free Press, 1990.

Lippman, S.A., and Richard P. Rumelt. Uncertain imitability: An analysis of interfirm differences in efficiency under competition. Bell Journal of Economics, 13 (Autumn), 1982.

Lipsey, Richard G., An introduction to positive economics, 3rd edition, Harper and Row, 1971.

Lowe, Janet. Bill Gates speaks. John Wiley & Sons Inc., 1998.

Lusztig, Peter A., and Bernhard I. Schwab. Managerial finance in a Canadian setting, 2nd edition. Butterworth & Co (Canada) Ltd., 1977.

March, J.G., and Z. Shapira. A primer on decision making: How decisions happen. New York: Free Press, 1994.

McGee, J., and T. Howard. Strategic groups: Theory research and taxonomy. Strategic Management Journal, 7, 1986.

Meredith, Jack R., and Samuel J. Mantel, Jr. Project management: A managerial approach, 3rd edition, John Wiley & Sons, Inc., 1995.

Milgrom, P. Roberts. The economics of modern manufacturing: Technology, strategy, and organization. American Economic Review, 80(3), 1995.

Miller, Roger LeRoy. Intermediate microeconomics: Theory, issues, and applications. McGraw-Hill Inc., 1978.

Mintzberg, H. The rise and fall of strategic planning. The Free Press: New York, 1994.

Mintzberg, H., B. Ahlstrand, and J. Lampel. Strategy safari: A guided tour through the wilds of strategic management. New York: Free Press, 1998.

NASA. Strategic management handbook, NASA February 2000.

Nelson, R.R. Why do firms differ and how much does it matter? Strategic Management Journal, 12, 1991.

Obringer, L.A. How the feds works (Economic indicators). http://money.howstuffworks.com/fed13.htm

Perks, Keith J., and Peter Bell. The management and strategic dilemmas in middle-sized firms. University of Brighton Business School, 2002.

Pfeffer, J., and G. Salanick. The external control of organizations. Harper, New York, 1978.

Plane, Donald A., and Gary A Kochenberger. Operations research for managerial decisions. Richard D. Irwin, Inc., 1973.

Porter, Michael E. Competitive advantage. The Free Press, New York, 1985.

Porter, Michael E. Competitive strategy. The Free Press, New York, 1980.

Porter, Michael E. Competitive strategy: Techniques for analysing industries and competitors. The Free Press, 1998 edition.

Porter, Michael E. From competitive advantage to corporate strategy. Harvard Business Review, May-June, 1987.

Porter, Michael E. What is strategy? Harvard Business Review, November-December 1996.

Prahalad, C.K., and Gary Hamel. The core competence of the corporation. Harvard Business Review, May–June 1990.

QuickMBA. Strategic management. www.quickmba.com

Robinson, Joan. The economics of imperfect competition. MacMillan Press, London, 1933.

Rumelt, R.P. How much does industry matter? Strategic Management Journal, March 1991.

Samuelson, Paul A., and Anthony Scott. Economics, 4th Canadian edition. McGraw-Hill Ryerson Limited, 1975.

Schoemaker, Paul J. How to link strategic vision to core capabilities. Sloan Management Review, 34 (Fall), 1992.

Scholl, Richard W. Organizational strategy. www.cba.uri.edu/Scholl/Notes/strategy.htm

Schmalensee, R. Do markets differ much? American Economic Review, 1985.

Schwalback, J. Profitability and market share: A reflection on the functional relationship. Strategic Management Journal, 1991.

Selznick, P. Leadership in administration. Row Peterson: Evaston ILL., 1957.

Senge, P. The fifth discipline. New York: Doubleday Currency, 1990.

Snow, C.C., and L.G Hrebiniak. Strategy, distinctive competence, and organizational performance. Administrative Science Quarterly, (25) 1980.

Sommers, Montrose S., and James G. Barnes. Fundamentals of marketing, 9th Canadian edition. McGraw-Hill Ryerson Limited, 2001.

Sommers, Montrose S., James C. Barnes, William J. Stanton, Michael J. Etzel, and Bruce J. Walker. Fundamentals of marketing, 9th Canadian edition. McGraw-Hill Ryerson Limited, 2001.

Stevenson, H. Defining corporate strengths and weaknesses. Sloan Management Review, Spring 1976.

Teece, D., G. Pisano, and A. Shuen. Dynamic capabilities and strategic management. Strategic Management Journal, 1997.

The Boston Consulting Group. This is BCG matrix. http://www.bcg.com

The Canadian Securities Institute. How to read financial statements. The Canadian Securities Institute, 1971 & 1973.

The key to ratios. www.kiplinger.com/features/archive/2002/11/keyratios.html

Thierauf, Robert J. and Robert C. Klekamp. Decision making through operations research, 2nd edition. John Wiley & Sons Inc., 1970.

Tzu, Sun. The art of war. http://classics.mit.edu/Tzu/artwar.html

Tzu, Sun. The art of war. http://kimsoft.com/polwar.htm

University of Cambridge Institute for Manufacturing. Manufacturing strategy and performance measurement. www.ifm.cam.ac.uk

Van Horne, James C. Financial management and policy, 2nd edition, Prentice-Hall Inc., 1971.

Walker. Fundamentals of marketing, 7th Canadian edition. McGraw-Hill Ryerson Limited, 2001.

Waring, G. Industry differences in the persistence of firm-specific returns. American Economic Review, December, 86, 1996.

Welch, Glen A., and Robert N. Anthony. Fundamentals of financial accounting. Richard D. Irwin, Inc., 1974.

Wernerfelt B. A resource-based view of the firm. Strategic Management Journal, 5, 1984.

Williams, Jeffrey R. How sustainable is your competitive advantage. California Management Review, Spring 1992.

Woodcock, Patrick C., and Paul W. Beamish. Concepts in strategic management, sixth edition. McGraw-Hill Ryerson Limited, 2003.

About the Author

The author has worked in many organizations, including a major Canadian bank and other multi-national corporations. He has observed first hand the performance of different companies that were clients of the bank. He saw how companies with effective business strategies performed and those without business strategies suffered the consequences, especially during economic downturn. The author has observed that executives, managers, and business owners constantly struggle with the challenge of figuring out what they have to do to earn higher profits, increase market share, achieve above-average returns, or increase growth. This convinced the author of the importance of a business strategy.

The author has also lived this experience as an entrepreneur by starting and owning a consulting firm of which he was the President and CEO. The author was a former Senior Advisor in the federal Government of Canada. He is now the President and CEO of GlobaStrat (www.globastrat.com). His experiences in Africa, Europe, and in North America convinced him that these struggles are not unique and are universal to the world of business. The author's passion for strategy comes from observing his father who was an entrepreneur and a King in a state in Ghana.

The author has an MBA (master of business administration) and an MPA (master of public administration). He appears as an occasional guest speaker at the MBA program (University of Ottawa School of Management).

How to order from the Publisher

To order copies of this book in bulk, call Author House at 1-888-519-5121 or visit www.globastrat.com.

www.ingramcontent.com/pod-product-compliance
Lightning Source LLC
Chambersburg PA
CBHW032001170526
45157CB00002B/495

* 9 7 8 1 4 2 0 8 6 9 1 8 7 *